Classro‹

M000306543

Classroom discussion is a concept familiar across the field of education and is often employed to support students' comprehension of text. Edited by a leading expert on classroom discussion, this book situates the topic within the broader context of educational psychology research and theory and brings it to a wider audience. Five chapters describe in detail the different approaches to discussion and provide recommendations for best practices and curricular materials for student success. This concise volume is designed for any education course that includes discussion in the curriculum and is indispensable for student researchers and both pre- and in-service teachers alike.

P. Karen Murphy is Professor of Education and Harry and Marion Royer Eberly Faculty Fellow in the Department of Educational Psychology, Counseling, and Special Education at The Pennsylvania State University, USA.

Ed Psych Insights

Series Editor: Patricia A. Alexander

EDITED BY P. KAREN MURPHY

Classroom Discussions in Education

Routledge
Taylor & Francis Group

NEW YORK AND LONDON

First published 2018
by Routledge
711 Third Avenue, New York, NY 10017

and by Routledge
2 Park Square, Milton Park, Abingdon, Oxon, OX14 4RN

Routledge is an imprint of the Taylor & Francis Group, an informa business

Library of Congress Cataloging-in-Publication Data
A catalog record for this book has been requested

ISBN: 978-1-138-04123-3 (hbk)
ISBN: 978-1-138-04121-9 (pbk)
ISBN: 978-1-315-17459-4 (ebk)

Typeset in Joanna MT
by Apex CoVantage, LLC

Contents

Acknowledgments

This research was supported by the Institute of Education Sciences, U.S. Department of Education, through Grant R305A130031 and the National Science Foundation, through Grant No. 1316347 to The Pennsylvania State University. Any opinions, findings, and conclusions or recommendations expressed are those of the author(s) and do not represent the views of the Institute, U.S. Department of Education, or the National Science Foundation.

Preface

In schools, talk is sometimes valued and sometimes avoided, but—and this is surprising—talk is rarely taught.

Lucy M. Calkins (p. 226)[1]

Historically, children in schools, public and private, have been taught that being a "good" student has a certain look. Good students are quiet and respectful, they raise their hands to ask the teacher a question, they stay seated in their chairs with their attention focused on the teacher or the task at hand, and perhaps more than anything else, they speak only when they are spoken to by the teacher or when they are instructed to speak, and even then, only in moderation. Indeed, good students are quiet students, and classrooms inhabited by silent, diligently working students are to be lauded. Such classrooms are the ones shown to touring parents or district administrators by the building principal. As a school-based intervention researcher, I have been escorted through these types of classrooms on multiple continents and in numerous countries. It seems that the "good" student and the "good" classroom enjoy somewhat of a universal acceptance among educational stakeholders. Further, the teachers in these types of classrooms are extolled and rewarded for their superior classroom management. Classroom management is so important, in fact, that many universities require prospective teachers to take at least one course that focuses on how to control their classroom. The central line of thought seems to be that students can think better and learn more in quiet classrooms.

Although there may be some merit to the idea that talk can be distracting to instruction and learning, the reality is that talk can also ignite and fuel students' thinking, particularly when the students play a central role in talk. It seems that students are far more likely to consider explanations given by a fellow student and to consider alternative perspectives forwarded by their classmates in comparison to explanations or alternatives offered by the classroom teacher.[2,3] Ironically, my anecdotal experience is that the challenges normally associated with classroom management actually dissipate when students, rather than teachers, do a majority of the talking in the classroom.[4] When meaningfully enacted, classroom talk, particularly small-group discussion, can foster students' critical-analytic thinking and reasoning, as well as comprehension of text and content learning.[5] Such skills serve as the foundation for students' ability to make meaning and reasoned decisions from text, transfer knowledge from one content area to another, and successfully integrate information across sources by making high-level inferences about the texts they have read.[6,7]

Consider a small group of fifth graders who are discussing a text about the sinking of the mighty RMS *Titanic*, in which many passengers lost their lives or those of loved ones. During the discussion a student poses the question, "Which do you think was worse, the sinking of the *Titanic* or the *Edmund Fitzgerald*?" The students soon become engaged in a lively debate over which event was more tragic or which sinking more unresolved. The open-ended question required that students' present various perspectives and weigh evidence in order to achieve some form of examined understanding. Moreover, the nature of the question required that the students make connections and weave together information from a past lesson about the Edmund Fitzgerald with the new information about the Titanic. This type of integration requires that students think about, around, and with a given text. Such thinking goes beyond basic text comprehension and is often referred to as high-level comprehension.[8] I would consider this type of text-based discussion as high quality because talk is being used as a tool for thinking and interthinking about, around, and with text.

In addition to the notion that talk can be used as a tool for thinking and collaborative interthinking by students,[9,10,8,11] the ability to exhibit one's thinking through discourse is a central part of career readiness.[12] Simply put, the workforce requires individuals to excel at oral and written communication. Whether debating the merits of a company innovation or communicating with colleagues or clients, individuals in the workforce must necessarily be adept at communication. The singular greatest challenge, as we have attempted to allude to and that Calkins so eloquently articulates,[1] is that talk has a tenuous existence in schools, and few, if any, teachers instruct students on the use of talk as a tool for thinking and the co-construction of ideas. That is, few teachers provide students with explicit instruction on ways to engage in talk that is useful or productive for learning, where the focus is not simply the quantity of talk, but also on the quality of their talk.[8] Although there are a number of explanations for the lack of explicit instruction, it is likely the case that teachers simply have not received formal instruction or professional development on fostering productive discussions with students. As a result, teachers resort to what they know: controlled classrooms with quiet, diligent students equal good instruction and learning.

As such, the purpose of this book is to provide educators with an overview of how talk can be used to promote students' learning in classrooms. Given the space limitations of this volume, we focus particularly on the use of small-group discussion to promote students' learning and high-level comprehension of text and content. Within this book we employ the term *high-level comprehension* to refer to students' ability to think critically and analytically about, around, and with text and content. The end goal of this type of high-quality, small-group discussion is not consensus among the group members, but rather that each student comes away from the discussion with a deeper, richer, more examined understanding of the text or content. Importantly, this volume is intended to be a practical, but brief, introduction to promoting learning about text and content through high-quality, small-group discussions in classrooms.

To achieve this overarching purpose, the book is divided into five chapters. Chapter 1 begins with a cursory overview of the theory undergirding small-group discussions as a pedagogy for enhancing learning. This basic overview of theory is buttressed with an exploration of how one's instructional frame sets the stage for small-group discussions. Chapter 2 follows with a more intensive look at the varied and evolving roles of teachers and students in small-group discussions. By comparison, Chapter 3 offers a detailed examination of the various factors that can affect the nature of small-group discussion, including the pedagogical decisions that teachers make in their classrooms and the contextual factors such as the reading ability of the group members. Once implemented, high-quality, small-group discussions give way to a number of positive student learning outcomes including enhanced cognitive processes like relational reasoning as well as individual student outcome improvements like written argumentation, as reviewed in Chapter 4. We end the volume in Chapter 5 with an exploration of our own small-group discussion approach called Quality Talk—a teacher-facilitated approach that promotes students' critical-analytic thinking about, around, and with text and content. Throughout the book we offer discourse excerpts and examples of real discussions from real classrooms as a way of providing concrete examples for the reader so that they may enact productive small-group discussions in their own classroom or work.

P. Karen Murphy
Professor of Education
Harry and Marion Royer Eberly Faculty Fellow
The Pennsylvania State University
October 2016

REFERENCES

1. Calkins, L. (2001). *The art of teaching reading*. New York, NY: Longman.

2. Alexander, P. A., & Dochy, F. J. (1995). Conceptions of knowledge and beliefs: A comparison across varying cultural and educational communities. *American Educational Research Journal, 32*(2), 413–442.

3. Murphy, P. K., Greene, J. A., Butler, A., & Criswell, B. A. (2015). *Integrating Quality Talk professional development to enhance professional vision and leadership for STEM teachers in high-need schools*. (Technical Report No. 2). University Park, PA: The Pennsylvania State University.

4. Murphy, P. K., Greene, J. A., & Firetto, C. M. (2014). *Quality Talk: Developing students' discourse to promote critical-analytic thinking, epistemic cognition, and high-level comprehension*. (Technical Report No. 1). University Park, PA: The Pennsylvania State University.

5. Murphy, P. K., Firetto, C. M., Wei, L., Li, M., & Croninger, R. M. (2016). What really works: Optimizing classroom discussions to promote comprehension and critical-analytic thinking. *Policy Insights from the Behavioral and Brain Sciences, 3*(1), 27–35. doi:10.1177/2372732215624215

6. Kintsch, W., & van Dijk, T. A. (1978). Toward a model of text comprehension and production. *Psychological Review, 85*(5), 363–394. doi:10.1037/0033-295x.85.5.363

7. Murphy, P. K., Rowe, M. L., Ramani, G., & Silverman, R. (2014). Promoting critical-analytic thinking in children and adolescents at home and in school. *Educational Psychology Review, 26*(4), 561–578. doi:10.1007/s10648-014-9281-3

8. Murphy, P. K., Wilkinson, I. A. G., Soter, A. O., Hennessey, M. N., & Alexander, J. F. (2009). Examining the effects of classroom discussion on

students' comprehension of text: A meta-analysis. *Journal of Educational Psychology, 101*(3), 740–764. doi:10.1037/a0015576

9. Brown, A. L., & Palincsar, A. S. (1987). *Reciprocal teaching of comprehension strategies: A natural history of one program for enhancing learning.* New York, NY: Ablex Publishing.

10. Mercer, N., Wegerif, R., & Dawes, L. (1999). Children's talk and the development of reasoning in the classroom. *British Educational Research Journal, 25*(1), 95–111. Retrieved from www.jstor.org/stable/1501934

11. Vygotsky, L. S. (1978). *Mind in society: The development of higher psychological processes.* Cambridge, MA: Harvard University Press.

12. National Governors Association Center for Best Practices & Council of Chief State School Officers. (2010). *Common core state standards.* Washington, DC: Authors.

One

Classroom Discussions

Building the Foundation for Productive Talk

*Rachel M. V. Croninger, Mengyi Li,
Chelsea Cameron, and P. Karen Murphy*

*Speech and action are part of one and the same complex psychological
function, directed toward the solution of the problem at hand.*

Lev Vygotsky (p. 25)[1]

Despite the rapid influx of various forms of electronic communication, talk remains integral to our daily lives. Talk guides everything from mundane activities like ordering coffee from your local barista or participating in a school club to making extremely complex decisions like whether to remain at a particular job or undergo a very dangerous surgical procedure. Talk serves as an essential form of communication, as well as a fundamental way of organizing our thoughts. In the same way, talk can also foster shared thinking or co-thinking about individual or community needs, ideas, or problems. We talk to trusted friends or classmates about complex or compelling questions as a means of exploring possibilities or examining evidence in the pursuit of solutions or resolutions. Given a truly complex or compelling question or issue, "inner-thinking" in the confines of one's own mind is rarely enough for most individuals. Rather, talk is the tool through which we think, consider, and weigh possibilities with others—the more difficult or vexing the problem, the more necessary it is to use talk as a tool for thinking.

Of course, this is not to say that all discussions result in efficient problem solving. Rather, talk may range from terribly unproductive at times to extremely productive at others; it is not the quantity of talk that determines its productivity, but the quality of talk that matters. For example, high school students discussing an after-school party during a small-group discussion when they should be discussing projectile motion is unproductive in terms of promoting students' learning. By comparison, high school students engaged in a small-group discussion in which they are evaluating competing scientific models of atomic structure can be fittingly considered high quality. The latter case is labeled high quality because the students are using their small-group discussion to examine their understandings of the various models of atoms and to evaluate the competing models using evidence and reasoning. This is exactly what Vygotsky meant when he suggested that talk and action are one and the same psychological function directed at the solution of a particular problem. For the aforementioned students, the problem required an exploration and comparison of the various atom models. Working together in a small group, these students employed talk as a tool for thinking and co-thinking or "interthinking" to solve the problem.

In the previous examples, it is fairly easy to determine that the on-task group of students is engaged in more high-quality talk than the off-task group of students who are discussing an after-school party. What's not overtly clear is "why" or "how" this type of talk, and the classroom discussion approaches that promote it, lead to enhanced learning outcomes. Answers to such questions can be found in the theories of learning that support discussion-based pedagogy. Indeed, an examination of various learning theories provides insight into the social and psychological mechanisms through which productive talk about text and content affects learners. Similarly, such theories shed light on how those participating in the talk experience play a role in the nature and outcomes of the discussion. In the sections that follow, we explore several theoretical frameworks that have been identified in the extant literature as providing the foundation for classroom discussions about text and content.

After briefly overviewing several prominent learning theories and their foundational underpinnings, we turn our attention to the ways in which the instructional frame influences a multitude of features of small-group discussion. As articulated by Vygotsky, the purpose of small-group discussion is to solve some problem or to achieve a given goal. As we have mentioned, solving a problem or achieving a goal through talk requires that the discussion be productive. In other words, effective discussions are those that serve a particular use by achieving an instructional goal. Importantly, not all approaches to discussion share the same instructional goal, and, therefore, not all approaches share common features, components, or instructional frames. As highlighted in the Preface to this volume, we are particularly interested in using *talk* to enhance students' critical-analytic thinking and reasoning about, around, and with text and content. Thus, our central focus of this chapter and those that follow will be ways to optimize small-group discussion so as to maximize students' deep, meaningful learning about text and content through quality talk.

THEORETICAL FOUNDATIONS

A scientific theory can best be understood as a system of empirically supported understandings about some real-world phenomena (e.g., reading comprehension). The system of principled understandings facilitates explanations of, predictions about, and interventions pertaining to the phenomena.[2] In this volume, our interest is focused on the use of small-group discourse to promote students' comprehension, critical-analytic thinking, and reasoning, as well as their ability to weigh and evaluate evidence (i.e., epistemic cognition). As such, we briefly turn to the world of learning theory as a way of providing an explanatory frame for how talk can be a tool for promoting students' high-level comprehension (i.e., critical-analytic thinking, reasoning, and epistemic cognition about, around, and with text and content). Specifically, we begin with social constructivist theory because talk is inherently social and interpersonal. We then turn to cognitive theory for a more in-depth look at how text or content is processed internally or intrapersonally. Finally, we conclude with a brief overview of social-cognitive theory that addresses the reciprocal interactions of person, behavior, and environment. Although each of the aforementioned theoretical frames is particularly broad, we offer only a narrow overview that is directly relevant to talk and high-level comprehension. Specifically, we describe how talk facilitates learning from text and content from a theoretical perspective. In addition, we also reflect on how theory guides instructional practice through the role of the teacher as a way of foreshadowing not only the second half of the present chapter, which explores instructional framing, but also a way to provide an explanatory frame for Chapter 2, which addresses teachers' and students' roles in productive discussion.

Social Constructivist

The central premise of social constructivist theory is that human development occurs in a social context, and, therefore, knowledge is constructed through interaction with objects in the environment. Such interactions would necessarily include talk or apprenticeship in a skill or trade. Importantly, the tools of the culture, including language, activities, and history, serve to mediate the ways in which individuals construct their understandings. In essence, knowledge and complex skills are not handed to learners in their final form. Rather, learners play an active role in building knowledge within the context of their environment by bringing together various pieces of information during social interactions. For example, a child reared in a remote, rural South African farming village would likely construct a worldview where apprenticeship into hard labor with one's hands is respected and valued—a worldview likely altogether different than a child raised in a wealthy suburb of New York City. Further, in this remote rural village, language and objects would reflect their meaning and value within that particular context, and necessarily, that meaning and value would vary as the culture and context varied. As a case in point, in a remote, rural South African farming community, *water* is a precious commodity and the term itself invokes cultural memories of drought, famine, and despair, as well as colonialism in which water rights were employed as a tool of oppression. Such an understanding of water would not likely be shared by the child from the wealthy New York City suburb.

Key among the theorists espousing a social constructivist view was a Russian psychologist and lawyer named Lev Vygotsky. Vygotsky theorized that psychological processes like comprehension or critical-analytic thinking developed first on an interpersonal level through interactions with others and things, and then they were internalized on a personal level. Vygotsky suggested that talk represented thought. As such, talk was a tool for thinking, through which students developed complex cognitive processes like high-level comprehension. Vygotsky suggested that talk was powerful because development was "more likely when one is required to explain, elaborate, or defend one's position to others, as well as to oneself; striving for an explanation often makes a learner integrate and elaborate in new ways" (p. 158).[1] Within classroom discussions, this type of development can be fostered through productive talk with peers and the teacher.

Importantly, the development of key discourse skills like asking questions, providing reasons and evidence, or posing challenges can be acquired directly through instruction and indirectly through apprenticeship by a more knowledgeable other within the context.

In a classroom, the more knowledgeable other may be a fellow classmate or the teacher. What is important about this individual is that she provides scaffolding for the student within what Vygotsky called the zone of proximal development (ZPD).[3] Unique to each learner, the ZPD represents a learner's potential growth when provided appropriate levels of scaffolding such that the student, with assistance, performs beyond their current ability level. As will be elaborated in Chapter 2, students and teachers can both serve as a more knowledgeable other through modeling, scaffolding, and facilitating classroom discussions about text and content. Through this discourse apprenticeship where high-quality talk is modeled and scaffolded for and by group members, learners internalize critical and analytic ways of thinking and reasoning.

Cognitive Theory

From a cognitive theoretical frame, learning is best understood as a relatively permanent change in one's behavioral potentiality. As such, the focus of the cognitive theory literature is on the acquisition, internal processing, recall, and use of knowledge. Within this volume, we are particularly interested in how engagement in productive, small-group discussions can promote knowledge acquisition, refinement, restructuring, retention, and use.[3,4] These processes are at the heart of text-based comprehension and content-area learning.

Given our focus on comprehension of text and content, we draw heavily on Kintsch's Construction Integration Model, which embraces the notion that readers construct mental representations of discourse that vary in complexity and, therefore, result in distinctive levels of comprehension ranging from shallow to deep (i.e., surface model, textbase model, and a situation model).[5,6] Within this model, mental representations can be understood as knowledge maps or webs composed of interconnected pieces of information. The tighter and more interconnected the web, the more likely that relevant information will be acquired, integrated, and retained for later use. From this perspective, discussion allows students to make meaning from text by supporting the construction of more complex representational maps or webs through productive discourse about, around, and with the text or content.[7]

Kintsch and colleagues emphasize three levels of text processing. The lowest level is the surface level, which involves the decoding of the actual words or phrases in the text and the formation of a verbatim representation of the text in working memory. Memory for the surface-level details of a text is short-lived. The next level is referred to as the textbase. At this level, the learner forms a semantic representation of the text where connections are made within and among the propositions or ideas in the text. When a text is coherent, the semantic associations among the propositions allow for global organization, inferences, and meaning making within the text. This level of processing enables students to respond to low-level or basic comprehension questions about the text, but they would likely struggle to think critically or analytically without integrating the text into their larger knowledge network.[8] Rather, the critical-analytic thinking and reasoning characterizing high-level comprehension requires an additional level of processing—a level that Kintsch referred to as the situation model.[5] At this level, the learner integrates their textbase model with their stores of prior knowledge. It is at this final level of text processing that learners would be able to critically and analytically weigh evidence or consider diverse lines of reasoning relative to their understanding of the text, as well as their own prior knowledge.

Arguably, productive discussions require that learners possess a surface-level understanding of the text, have formed a textbase of text or content, and have begun to consider the extent to which the textbase integrates with their prior knowledge. In essence, small-group discussions foster students' integration of the text or content and offer the opportunities to form and solidify their situation model. An important consideration is that while learners are forming situation models of the text or content through the discussion, they are simultaneously proceeding through the construction-integration process of the oral discourse as it unfolds. Given this colossal cognitive load, the teacher's role in scaffolding, monitoring, and facilitating becomes immensely important and complex. The teacher must monitor not just the group members' talk, but also think about what that talk represents in terms of students' cognitive processing and integration of the text or content during the discussion. Such a role is extremely challenging, which underscores the need for the teacher to facilitate rather than actively participate in the discussions.

Sociocognitive Theory

As the name suggests, sociocognitive theory takes both social and cognitive factors into account when exploring learning processes.[9] Albert Bandura is, perhaps, the best-known sociocognitive theorist. The heart of Bandura's theory is that the learner, her behavior, and the environment enjoy a reciprocally deterministic relationship.[10] In short, the internal characteristics of the learner (e.g., cognitive processing) influence the person's behavior, which then influences the environment or context, and the process necessarily feeds back on itself. Consider a classroom in which a student has previously received negative feedback about his math performance. The student processes and internalizes that information, which may propel him to work harder on math homework or, conversely, to work less because he does not believe in himself. The student's behavior will then influence how the teacher or other students in the environment respond, which will ultimately influence the student's self-perceptions. Rooted in this triadic reciprocation, Bandura proposed that environmental models were an extremely strong force in learning.[10] In essence, students learn through the observation of the behaviors and concomitant rewards and punishments of models in their environment. As a case in point, children first begin to learn to speak by mimicking the language of their caregivers.

In the early 1980s, Doise and Mugny turned their socio-cognitive lens on social interactions with a particular focus on conflict.[11] Most individuals who have taken part in social interactions have experienced social conflict or challenge. Rather than assume that such conflict is inherently negative, Doise and Mugny were interested in the extent to which social conflict or challenge paid cognitive dividends. What they found was that social conflict or challenge was a positive force in students' reorganization or elaboration of cognitive representations. In short, challenge on the social plane gave way to cognitive restructuring as well as stronger verbal substantiation of one's position. For example, consider a small-group discussion in which students are exploring why rainbows appear in radiator fluid. One student argues that water in the radiator fluid causes the rainbows because rainbows are contained in water droplets, which is why, he argues, rainbows can be seen on rainy days. A fellow student, unsure of the soundness of the explanation, counters the student's justification with a scientific explanation of rainbows and light reflected within a water droplet. The student who is challenged by his peer is far more likely to alter his understanding than if he simply read a scientific explanation from a textbook. In this way, discussions that involve elements of challenge are more likely to foster students' deep, meaningful processing of text and content through the restructuring and elaboration of their understanding (i.e., prior knowledge).

From this perspective, the teacher is a central actor in the environment of the learner. First, the teacher provides explicit modeling and feedback to the learner within small-group discussions. By doing so, the teacher helps the learner acquire essential knowledge, skills, and abilities foundational to high-level comprehension. For example, by modeling critical-analytic thinking, the teacher creates a space where those in the group can observe and learn. Second, the teacher serves to facilitate the discourse and challenge the understandings, positions, or perspectives of those in the group. In doing so, the teacher encourages knowledge acquisition, refinement, restructuring, and use. Indeed, as shown by prior research, students exposed to or participating in this type of social conflict or challenge will enhance their understandings.

What each of these theories offers is an explanatory frame for how and why talk is a vehicle for deep, critical-analytic thinking, reasoning, and interthinking. Taken together, these theories serve to guide instructional discourse practices that promote high-level comprehension. However, as we suggested previously, high-level comprehension is not the proposed outcome goal of every approach to discussion. As we will share in the section that follows, goals and purposes for small-group discussion vary by the approach. Further, as might be expected, the goal of the discussion influences the ways in which the discussion is framed through instruction.[12] Specifically, the section that follows explicates the instructional frame that sets the stage for high-quality discussions aimed at enhancing comprehension and critical-analytic thinking and reasoning.

INSTRUCTIONAL FRAMING

In recent decades, classroom discussions have become a prominent theme in the literature on text-based comprehension and learning. A number of discussion approaches have emerged and appear to be effective in stimulating intellectual responses to text in diverse learning contexts (e.g., Collaborative Reasoning, Philosophy for Children, and Questioning the Author).[13,14,15] In order to better understand the nature and effectiveness of various approaches to discussion, Murphy and colleagues conducted a meta-analysis of relevant empirical studies and found that not all approaches to discussion are equally effective at generating productive talk.[12] Further, increases in student talk do not necessarily lead to enhanced learning about text and content. Indeed, the various components of instructional framing influence the discussion and, consequently, the resulting learning outcomes. In order to optimize the valuable class time allocated to small-group discussions, it is vitally important that teachers consider all aspects of instructional framing, as each one will necessarily influence the quality of student talk.

Based on their analysis of nine discussion approaches, Wilkinson and colleagues highlighted a set of parameters essential for conducting small-group discussions.[16] The parameters pertained to a set of decisions that, in essence, defined the instructional frame for the discussion. These parameters include but are not limited to:

- What is the adopted stance toward the text (i.e., efferent, expressive, or critical-analytic)?
- Who has control of the turns?
- Who holds interpretive authority?
- Who chooses the text?
- What genre is used?
- When does reading occur (i.e., before, during, or after the discussion)?

- How are groups formed?
- If ability grouping is used, is the group homogeneous or heterogeneous in ability?
- Is the discussion teacher-led or student-led?

The answers to these questions are influenced by the goals and purposes embraced by various discussion approaches, thus defining their instructional frame. Importantly, Wilkinson and colleagues[16] proposed an *ideal* instructional frame for discussions that aim to promote high-level comprehension and critical-analytic thinking; that is, the pedagogical goal we set forth in the Preface. Here we briefly describe the ideal instructional frame and how this set of conditions forms the foundation for high-quality talk before, during, and after discussion.

Prior to the discussion, the teacher selects a text for the students to read. The students read the text and develop a basic understanding of it. As highlighted in the cognitive theory section, it is important that readers come to the discussion with an explicit textbase level of comprehension that can serve as the foundation for more sophisticated, critical, and analytic thinking about, around, and with text. Within this framework, students also engage in pre-discussion activities designed to activate their prior knowledge related to the text, such as personal or cultural experiences, domain or topic knowledge, and understanding of text feature or structure.[17] Explicit instruction and practice are also needed for students to learn how to generate questions that are more likely to facilitate high-level comprehension (i.e., *authentic questions*; see Chapter 5 for more information) as well as how to make reasoned arguments. These pre-discussion activities prime students' prior knowledge and better situate them to benefit from the subsequent small-group discussions.

During the discussions, instead of taking a predominant role, the teacher shares control with the students. Specifically, the teacher has control over the topic of discussion, whereas the students have control over turns. It should be noted that in the early stages of discussions, it is important for the teacher to model and support critical and analytic thinking through various scaffolding moves (see Chapter 2 for more information). Once students internalize these ways of thinking and are able to use them to support their own thinking,[18] the teacher gradually releases control of the discussion so that students increasingly take on more responsibility and interpretative authority.[19] Shared control is beneficial for establishing an open participation structure during discussions and allows students to co-construct understandings of the text and content with peers, leading to more fruitful learning outcomes.[16] In addition, as will be expanded later, students are better positioned to adopt a critical-analytic orientation when they are knowledge-driven, engaged, and personally connected to the text.

After the discussion, the teacher provides immediate feedback regarding students' performance during the discussion.[17] Students have opportunities to reflect on their discourse practices and set specific goals for future improvement, such as asking more authentic questions. Post-discussion activities, such as writing an argumentative essay, foster the transfer of thinking and reasoning from oral discourse to written discourse and from the group level to the individual level, which further strengthens and solidifies students' learning about text and content.[20] Taken together, the conditions set forth over the three phases of classroom discussion reveal an instructional frame that is likely to stimulate high-quality talk and high-level comprehension of text. In the remainder of this chapter, the focus will shift toward a deeper exploration of the impact of the stance toward text on discussions, as Murphy and colleagues found that much of the variance in student comprehension and learning outcomes was due to the literacy stance espoused by different discussion approaches.[12]

Guidance for Practitioners

- Careful consideration should be given to how each condition of the instructional frame (e.g., stance, who holds interpretive authority, or text genre) will affect student talk during discussion.
- Discussion conditions should be thoughtfully established so that they scaffold productive talk and meaningful learning.
- Explicit instruction and practice is necessary for teachers and students to feel comfortable about the gradual release of control, responsibility, and interpretive authority.

Stances Toward Text

The notion of stance originated from Rosenblatt's transactional theory of reading, which focuses on readers' responses to literary work. Different readers approach the text with different goals and, accordingly, they could have different *takeaways* depending on the purpose of the reading event. According to Rosenblatt, an individual either consciously or unconsciously adopts a predominant stance toward a selected text.[21] The stance then guides the individual's approach toward the text (e.g., knowledge gathering or enjoyment) and influences her understandings, particularly when multiple interpretations of the text are available.

The concept of stance was later extended to literature on classroom discussions. As part of an instructional frame, stance toward text should align with the goals set for students. Clearly the espoused stance greatly influences the pedagogical decisions that teachers make as well as the benchmarks for success (e.g., high-level comprehension). For instance, if the goal of discussion is to primarily locate and recall particular information (i.e., an *efferent stance*), then students should be supported to comprehend what is explicitly stated in the text; if the goal is to foster a reader-focused response (i.e., an *expressive stance*), then students should be encouraged to build personal, emotive connections to the text during discussions; and if the goal is to provoke critical thinking and reasoning about, around, and with text (i.e., a *critical-analytic stance*), then the discussions should give rise to students' engaged querying and the interrogation of text in search of its underlying arguments, assumptions, or beliefs.[16]

The following sections briefly overview the nature of each of the three stances with an exemplar discussion approach, as well as attempt to illustrate how they are enacted by teachers or researchers in practice with transcripts collected from authentic classroom discussions. The prominent approaches to discussion that have been identified in the extant literature can be broadly categorized into each of the three stances toward text: efferent, expressive, or critical-analytic.[12] However, it is worth noting that some of the discussion approaches may enact secondary or tertiary goals that correspond with multiple stances. For instance, a number of approaches that espouse a critical-analytic stance (e.g., Collaborative Reasoning and Quality Talk) may also support the searching of text for information as well as the building of affective connections to the text, so as to better enable learners to critically examine the underlying argument and evidence presented in the text.[12] As such, the discussion approach that we chose as an exemplar for each stance was identified based on its primary goals.

Efferent Stance Toward Text

In Rosenblatt's transactional theory, a reader adopting a predominantly efferent stance will be concerned with what will be retained as the *residue* after the reading event, such as acquiring and retrieving information. An extreme example of taking an efferent stance can be illustrated by "a man who has accidentally swallowed a poisonous liquid and is rapidly reading the label on the bottle to learn the antidote" (p. 1372).[22] In this case, the man's attention is so absorbed in extracting information from the text in order to survive that he excludes anything other than the text's explicitly stated information. Less extreme examples of taking an efferent stance might be individuals reading a newspaper, a manual, or a legal brief.

Approaches to discussion that give prominence to an efferent stance emphasize reading to acquire and retrieve textual information, and thus they entail a text-focused response from the reader.[23] For instance, Questioning the Author (QtA) is a teacher-led discussion approach that focuses on engaging students to actively construct meaning from written text and question the author as they read.[24] QtA is characterized as favoring an efferent stance toward text and is deeply rooted in a constructivist perspective.[25] Specifically, prior to conducting a QtA discussion, the teacher explicitly explains to students that a text is always written by an author who is imperfect and falliable.[26] Hence, the problems they experience while reading are not necessarily due to their lack of reading proficiency. Rather, they could be attributable to an author's insufficiency.[24] During a QtA discussion, the teacher guides a whole class of students to read the text together and pauses at each section to initiate queries, which are generic questions designed to facilitate meaning construction from the text. Examples of queries are "What is the author trying to say?" or "How does that connect with what the author already told us?" (p. 389).[24] Students are expected to respond actively to the queries and share thoughts as they build mental representations of the text. Throughout the discussion, the teacher employs various teacher moves (e.g., modeling, marking, or paraphrasing) to encourage text-focused responses and to assist students in the process of meaning making from text.[26]

In their meta-analysis, Murphy and colleagues found that, on average, efferent discussion approaches increased student talk and had mixed effects on teacher talk (i.e., some decreased teacher talk, whereas others increased it).[12] Specifically, QtA discussions only had a moderate, positive effect on student talk and slightly increased teacher talk. This finding is not surprising, as teachers take a predominant role in QtA discussions and students do not control the flow of talk. Findings also indicated that discussion approaches like QtA that emphasize an efferent stance lead to sizable comprehension gains due to their focus on knowledge gathering. However, it should be noted that many of the studies examined were single-group design studies (i.e., pre- and post-test without control groups) and, therefore, it is unclear how students' comprehension gains compare to students who did not experience the discussions. Thus, more research with multiple-group designs is needed to verify the effects of efferent approaches on student reading comprehension.

The two discourse excerpts shown in Figures 1.1 and 1.2 were collected from a high school science class and a fifth-grade language arts class, respectively. In both cases, the teacher initiated the conversation with a recall question, trying to assess students' factual understanding or knowledge acquired as a result of reading. The question had a preconceived answer and the student managed to provide the *correct* answer after retrieving specific concepts or details from the text. In the end, the teachers gave positive feedback verbally ("Yes! That is right!" and "Perfect"),

Topic: *Nuclear Fission*

Turn	Speaker	Transcribed Talk
1.	Mrs. Vriend	How do you know nitrogen is unreactive?
2.	Mallory	Because it's a triple bond.
3.	Ms. Vriend	Yes! That is right!

Figure 1.1 Excerpt from a small-group discussion in a high school science classroom

Turn	Speaker	Transcribed Talk
	Text: *Dear Mr. Henshaw*	
1.	Mr. Quarles	Why didn't Lee hang out much with his dad?
2.	Robert	Because his Dad is a truck driver, he has to drive to a lot of different places around the country.
3.	Mr. Quarles	Perfect!

Figure 1.2 Excerpt from a small-group discussion in a fifth-grade classroom

but such feedback could also be nonverbal (e.g., gesture or nod). Due to their emphasis on explicit textual information, both of the excerpts illustrate what a classroom discussion would look like if teachers enacted an efferent stance toward text.

Expressive Stance Toward Text

A reader holding a predominantly expressive stance is attuned to gaining a *lived through experience* from reading and values the *private* and emotive aspects of textual meaning.[21] Originally, Rosenblatt made distinctions between an *efferent* stance and an *aesthetic* stance. Yet, the term *aesthetic* was later substituted by *expressive* in the literature on classroom discussions, due to the fact that very few discussion approaches actually obtained truly aesthetic responses from readers.[27] Thus, in order to better describe a reader's response to text during classroom discussions, Soter and her colleagues used the alternative term *expressive* to account for a reader's "spontaneous, emotive connection to all aspects of the textual experience" (p. 374).[27]

As a case in point, Book Club (BC) is a discussion approach that encourages an expressive stance toward text.[12] BC is the core element of an integrated literature-based program that consists of four components: reading, writing, discussion, and direct instruction.[28] These four components are geared toward supporting student-led, small-group discussions, and the primary goal of discussion is to provide students with a context within which they could engage in meaningful conversations about text and elicit reader-focused response.[28] BC is established from a social constructivist perspective,[29,30] which views learning as both socially based and integrated. The procedure for conducting BC discussions is as follows. First, students read a selected text and write personal responses to the text in the form of journals or reading logs. During the BC discussions, students form heterogeneous groups and share with one another their personal reactions to the text using journals or reading logs.[31] Following the discussion, students often participate in *community share*,[28] which is a teacher-led, whole-class discussion that invites students to share ideas from BC discussions and to relate them to personal feelings and experiences. Direct instruction is provided throughout the program for varied purposes, such as introducing new reading strategies, teaching literacy elements, or discussing language conventions.[28]

According to Murphy and colleagues,[12] very few empirical studies have been conducted to examine the effects of expressive discussion approaches on individual reading comprehension. Some evidence in the BC literature shows that students are more inclined to share their thoughts about the text and make more connections to their personal experiences during discussions.[32] Also, by comparing the results of pertinent research, Murphy and colleagues found that although BC discussions only minimally increased student talk, they do influence students' reading metacognition (e.g., self-questioning and summarizing). However, many studies that have examined expressive discussion approaches did not measure comprehension or critical thinking.[12] Indeed, the lack of findings on comprehension and critical thinking is not surprising, as the primary goal of such approaches is to create an environment for students to share their personal responses and to foster their spontaneous, emotive connections to the literacy work. What we know from these analyses, however, is that on average an expressive stance increases the amount of student talk. However, more research is necessary to measure the quality of student talk produced and its impact on text comprehension.

Figure 1.3 contains an example of classroom discussion that could occur within an instructional frame promoting an expressive stance toward text. In the excerpt, two fifth-grade students discuss feelings of loneliness based on a story about a lone cowboy. Nicholas initiated the discussion by speculating about a cowboy's likely emotional state, and Maria elaborated on his statement by making a connection to her own life. Drawing on her understanding of her parents' different personalities, Maria was able to build personal and emotive connection to the text—such connection would enrich Maria's meaning-making process and deepen both her understanding of the story as well as her peer's.

Text: *Black Cowboy, Wild Horses*

Turn	Speaker	Transcribed Talk
1.	Nicholas	I also think of a cowboy's life as maybe being lonely. Like Bob
		[the cowboy in the story] had Warrior [his horse], I guess...
		as a friend. It just seems like they are off on their own a lot.
2.	Maria	You have to [be] an inside person [to be on your own a lot],
		like, can't want to deal with people. Like, my Mom is a people
		person but my Dad is more, like, inside of himself, like he
		likes to think.
3.	Nicholas	Oh, an introvert! Ok.

Figure 1.3 Excerpt from a small-group discussion in a fifth-grade classroom

Critical-Analytic Stance Toward Text

In an effort to more fully capture the ways that readers approach a text, Wade, Thompson, and Watkins proposed a third stance, *critical-analytic*, to add to Rosenblatt's taxonomy.[33] Their assertion was based on a study in which they compared the responses of two groups of adult viewers to a documentary video on the Civil War. They found that professional historians responded from a more critical perspective by querying and interrogating the content and source of the video, whereas non-professional viewers responded from a more appreciative view without questioning the accuracy of the presented information. Based on their findings, the *critical-analytic* stance was later employed by researchers to capture the full range of readers' responses in text-based discussions.[16,34] In text-based discussions, a critical-analytic stance requires the reader to not only engage with a querying mind and question the text, but also make reasoned, evidence-based responses to unsolved issues, problems, or underlying arguments inferred from the text.[27]

Collaborative Reasoning (CR) is a teacher-facilitated, small-group discussion approach that is representative of approaches encouraging a critical-analytic stance toward text.[12,34] CR is deeply rooted in a sociocultural perspective and reflects the Vygotskian idea of internalization.[35] That is, all higher cognitive processes of one's thought should originate from "the collective life . . . in the form of argumentation and only later develop into reflection" (p. 157).[36] CR is intended to be intellectually stimulating and personally engaging for all participating students.[35] The procedure for a CR discussion is as follows. First, the teacher has students silently read a short story that contains an unsolved issue with multiple alternative solutions (e.g., a moral dilemma). The teacher then starts the discussion by posing a *big question* that is related to the unsolved issue.[34] Each student should pick a position and take turns to respond to the central question, ideally, with reasoned discourse. Drawing on their personal experiences, preexisting knowledge, and the text, students are encouraged to critically examine reasons and evidence, to challenge others' points of view, and to consider alternatives.[34] CR discussions follow an open participation structure, that is, students do not have to raise their hands or be called upon by the teacher before they speak, provided they do not interrupt others.[13] During the discussion, the teacher gradually steps back and takes more of a facilitative role.[18] The ultimate goal for CR discussions is not about reaching consensus but providing students with the opportunities to engage in reasoned argumentation and use it as a model for critical thinking.[35]

Murphy and colleagues found that critical-analytic discussion approaches such as CR greatly increased student talk and decreased teacher talk compared to traditional recitations.[12,37] During CR discussions, for example, students were also found to engage more with high-level thinking skills, such as making elaborations, challenging others' ideas, and providing evidence to support their utterances.[35] However, other than group talk and critical thinking skills, students' comprehension gains as individual outcomes have been sparse. These findings further support the contention that increased student talk does not necessarily lead to improved comprehension of text. Rather, a specific kind of high-quality talk is necessary for promoting students' comprehension.

Figure 1.4 show an excerpt of a discussion that embodies a critical-analytic stance in a science class. In this excerpt, a group of high school students discusses how airbags increase the time it takes for a person to hit a steering wheel during a car accident. In order to better understand this phenomenon, both Melissa and Andrea integrated information from multiple sources (i.e., the text, their personal experiences, and the media) to support their claims. The students were seemingly engaged

Turn	Speaker	Transcribed Talk
		Topic: *Force and Motion*
1.	Andrea	How does the airbag increase the time it takes for you to hit the steering wheel?
2.	Jonas	Since it is deflating, you're still technically moving forward. So, when you hit it you are moving forward still, instead of hitting the steering wheel, and then your force is bounced back and you fly back. So, instead of that, you do like a slower forward motion.
3.	Melissa	Well, in the video the person did hit the airbag and bounce back, not like how you are describing.
4.	Jonas	Well, I guess it would depend on how fast you are going.
5.	Andrea	Well, I think in the one video it didn't deflate at all, so that's why they bounced back. But, if it was deflating when you hit it, you would go forward still, but not as fast as without an airbag there.

Figure 1.4 Excerpt from a discussion in a high school classroom

in a problem-solving activity whereby the solution could not be found directly in the text. In searching for the solution, they made public their thoughts, considered alternative perspectives, critically examined reasons and evidence, and thus co-constructed knowledge about the scientific phenomenon.

Importantly, the stances that we use to categorize diverse approaches to discussion are not necessarily mutually exclusive. Indeed, it is impossible for discussion to foster a truly critical-analytic stance toward text without simultaneously drawing support from both an affective and knowledge-driven engagement. At least a moderate degree of emphasis on the efferent and expressive stances is necessary for fostering a critical-analytic orientation to the text (see Figure 1.5).

The juxtaposition of three exemplar approaches as well as authentic classroom transcripts allow us to discern the relations between the stance toward text and the other components

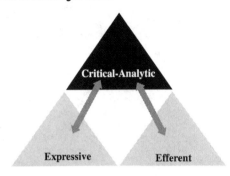

Figure 1.5 Representation of how the critical-analytic stance is supported by the expressive and efferent stances

within the instructional frame. Specifically, the stance enacted in the discussions seems to relate to the distribution of control between teacher and students.[16] Teachers seem to have the greatest control in discussions that espouse an efferent stance. On the contrary, students seem to have the greatest control in discussions that advocate an expressive stance. Further, the discussion that gives prominence to a critical-analytic stance seems to promote shared control between teacher and students. As illustrated earlier in the ideal instructional frame, it is this shared control between teacher and students that is key to prompting high-level comprehension and critical-analytic thinking.

Guidance for Practitioners

- It is important to use an efferent stance to ensure basic comprehension, an expressive stance to enhance students' interest in the discussion, and a critical-analytic stance to stimulate students' critical-analytic thinking and reasoning.
- Just as students are taught about text genre, it is also valuable to teach students about how one's stance toward a text influences what is gained during the reading process. This will

enable students to better monitor their own stance toward texts as well as the alignment of their stance with the established goals for reading.

CODA

Talk is a powerful tool. A tool that students can use in and out of the classroom to think critically, reason, and solve problems together. Vygotsky held that such "interthinking" was the root of talk's power; that splitting the cognitive burden allows students to accomplish complex cognitive tasks beyond their ability level and subsequently internalize such skills. Alternatively, cognitive and sociocognitive theorists focus on how social interaction (e.g., discussion) can lead to the dynamic restructuring and elaboration of students' cognitive representations of text and content. Each theory asserts that talk is a powerful tool for thinking; however, research has shown that not all talk is equally effective in promoting high-level comprehension, complex reasoning, and learning.[12] Consequently, one of the challenges in using discussion-based pedagogy is employing an instructional frame that does not simply increase the amount of student talk but also fosters high-quality talk.

What teachers and students do before, during, and after a discussion will influence the productivity and utility of student talk. Therefore, it is important to employ an instructional frame that scaffolds talk to meet the unique goals of each individual classroom and distinct discussion group. Of the conditions included in the instructional frame, stance accounts for the most variance in terms of efficacy of an approach for promoting high-level comprehension and critical-analytic thinking.[12] However, it is important to note that no stance is inherently better than another; they simply serve different purposes. An efferent stance is very text oriented and focuses on locating and retrieving textual information; an expressive stance fosters personal connections to the text and enjoyment in reading; and a critical-analytic stance stimulates students' critical-analytic thinking and reasoning. In this way, the effectiveness of a discussion approach is largely influenced by its espoused stance toward text. Practitioners should adopt the stance that aligns best with their discussion goals while also incorporating elements of the remaining two stances to ensure that students achieve the many learning goals set forth.

REFERENCES

1. Vygotsky, L. S. (1978). Mind in society: The development of higher psychological processes. Cambridge, MA: Harvard University Press.

2. Murphy, P. K., & S. L. Knight. (2016). Exploring a century of advancements in the science of learning. In P. A. Alexander, F. L. Levine, & W. Tate (Vol. Eds.), Education research: A century of discovery, 40, 402–456. doi:10.3102/0091732X16677020

3. Murphy, P. K., Wilkinson, I. A. G., & Soter, A. O. (2011). Instruction based on discussion. In R. Mayer & P. A. Alexander (Eds.), Handbook of research on learning and instruction (pp. 382–407). New York, NY: Routledge. doi:10.4324/9780203839089.ch19

4. Piaget, J. (1928). The child's conception of the world. London: Routledge and Kegan Paul.

5. Kintsch, W. (1988). The role of knowledge in discourse comprehension: A construction-integration model. Psychological Review, 95(2), 163–182. doi:10.1037/0033295X.95.2.163

6. Kintsch, W. (1998). Comprehension: A paradigm for cognition. New York, NY: Cambridge University Press.

7. McKeown, M. G., Beck, I. L., & Blake, R. G. (2009). Rethinking reading comprehension instruction: A comparison of instruction for strategies and content approaches. Reading Research Quarterly, 44(3), 218–253. doi:10.1598/RRQ.44.3.1

8. McNamara, D. S., & Kintsch, W. (1996). Learning from texts: Effects of prior knowledge and text coherence. Discourse Processes, 22(3), 247–288. doi:10.1080/01638539609544975

9. Almasi, J. F. (1995). The nature of fourth graders' sociocognitive conflicts in peer-led and teacher-led discussions of literature. Reading Research Quarterly, 30(3), 314–351. doi:10.2307/747620

10. Bandura, A. (1977). *Social learning theory*. Englewood Cliffs, NJ: Prentice Hall.

11. Doise, W., & Mugny, G. (1984). *The social development of the intellect*. Oxford, England: Pergamon Press. doi:10.1016/c2009-0-11024-3

12. Murphy, P. K., Wilkinson, I. A. G., Soter, A. O., Hennessey, M. N., & Alexander, J. F. (2009). Examining the effects of classroom discussion on students' comprehension of text: A meta-analysis. *Journal of Educational Psychology*, 101(3), 740–764. doi:10.1037/a0015576

13. Anderson, R. C., Chinn, C., Waggoner, M., & Nguyen, K. (1998). Intellectually stimulating story discussions. In K. O. Jean & F. Lehr (Eds.), *Literacy for all: Issues in teaching and learning* (pp. 170–186). New York, NY: Guilford Press.

14. Sharp, A. M. (1995). Philosophy for Children and the development of ethical values. *Early Child Development and Care*, 107, 45–55. doi:10.1080/0300443951070106

15. Beck, I. L., & McKeown, M. G. (2006). *Improving comprehension with Questioning the Author: A fresh and expanded view of a powerful approach*. New York, NY: Scholastic.

16. Wilkinson, I. A. G., Soter, A. O., & Murphy, P. K. (2010). Developing a model of Quality Talk about literary text. In M. G. McKeown & L. Kucan (Eds.), *Bringing reading research to life* (pp. 142–169). New York, NY: Guilford Press.

17. Murphy, P. K., Firetto, C. M., Wei, L., Li, M., & Croninger, R. M. V. (2016). What really works: Optimizing classroom discussions to promote comprehension and critical-analytic thinking. *Policy Insights from the Behavioral and Brain Sciences*, 1, 1–9. doi:10.1177/2372732215624215

18. Jadallah, M., Anderson, R. C., Nguyen-Jahiel, K., Miller, B. W., Kim, I. H., Kuo, L. J., & Wu, X. (2011). Influence of a teacher's scaffolding moves during child-led small-group discussions. *American Educational Research Journal*, 48(1), 194–230. doi:10.3102/0002831210371498

19. Mercer, N. (2000). *Words and minds: How we use language to think together*. London: Routledge. doi:10.4324/9780203464984

20. Firetto, C. M., Murphy, P. K., Greene, J. A., Li, M., & Wei, L. (2015, August). *Enhancing students' written argumentation through Quality Talk*. Paper presented at the Biennial Meeting of the European Association for Research on Learning and Instruction, Limassol, Cyprus.

21. Rosenblatt, L. M. (1978). *The reader, the text, and the poem: The transactional theory of the literary work*. Carbondale, IL: Southern Illinois University Press. doi:10.2307/376410

22. Rosenblatt, L. M. (2005). *Making meaning with texts: Selected essays.* Portsmouth, NH: Heinemann Educational Books.

23. Chinn, C. A., Anderson, R. C., & Waggoner, M. A. (2001). Patterns of discourse in two kinds of literature discussion. *Reading Research Quarterly, 36,* 378–411. doi:10.1598/RRQ.36.4.3

24. Beck, I. L., McKeown, M. G., Sandora, C., Kucan, L., & Worthy, J. (1996). Questioning the author: A yearlong classroom implementation to engage students with text. *The Elementary School Journal, 96,* 385–414. doi:10.2307/1001863

25. Anderson, R. C. (1977). The notion of schemata and the educational enterprise. In R. C. Anderson, R. J. Spiro, & W. E. Montague (Eds.), *Schooling and the acquisition of knowledge* (pp. 415–431). Hillsdale, NJ: Erlbaum.

26. Beck, I. L., McKeown, M. G., Hamilton, R. L., & Kucan, L. (1997). *Questioning the author: An approach for enhancing student engagement with text.* Newark, DE: International Reading Association.

27. Soter, A. O., Wilkinson, I. A., Murphy, P. K., Rudge, L., Reninger, K., & Edwards, M. (2008). What the discourse tells us: Talk and indicators of high-level comprehension. *International Journal of Educational Research, 47(6),* 372–391. doi:10.1016/j.ijer.2009.01.001

28. Raphael, T. E., & McMahon, S. I. (1994). Book Club: An alternative framework for reading instruction. *The Reading Teacher, 48(2),* 102–116. doi:10.2307/20201379

29. Gavelek, J. R. (1986). The social context of literacy and schooling: A developmental perspective. In T. E. Raphael (Ed.), *The contexts of school-based literacy* (pp. 3–26). New York, NY: Random House.

30. Tharp, R., & Gallimore, R. (1988). *Rousing minds to life: Teaching, learning and schooling in social context.* Cambridge, MA: Cambridge University Press. doi:10.1017/cbo9781139173698

31. Goatley, V. J., Brock, C. H., & Raphael, T. E. (1995). Diverse learners participating in regular education "Book Clubs." *Reading Research Quarterly, 30(3),* 352–380. doi:10.2307/747621

32. Kong, A., & Fitch, E. (2002). Using Book Club to engage culturally and linguistically diverse learners in reading, writing, and talking about books. *The Reading Teacher, 56(4),* 352–362. Retrieved from www.jstor.org/stable/20205209

33. Wade, S., Thompson, A., & Watkins, W. (1994). The role of belief systems in authors' and readers' constructions of texts. In P. A. Alexander & R. Garner (Eds.), *Beliefs about text and instruction with text* (pp. 265–293). Hillsdale, NJ: Lawrence Erlbaum Associates Publishers.

34. Waggoner, M., Chinn, C., Yi, H., & Anderson, R. C. (1995). Collaborative reasoning about stories. *Language Arts, 72*(8), 582–589. doi:10.2307/41482243

35. Chinn, C. A., Anderson, R. C., & Waggoner, M. A. (2001). Patterns of discourse in two kinds of literature discussion. *Reading Research Quarterly, 36*(4), 378–411. doi:10.1598/rrq.36.4.3

36. Vygotsky, L. S. (1981). The genesis of higher mental functions. In J. V. Wertsch (Ed.), *The concept of activity in psychology* (pp. 144–188). Armonk, NY: M. E. Sharpe.

37. Mehan, H. (1979). *Learning lessons: The social organization of classroom instruction.* Cambridge, MA: Harvard University Press. doi:10.4159/harvard.9780674420106

38. Wineburg, S. S. (1991). Historical problem solving: A study of the cognitive processes used in the evaluation of documentary and pictorial evidence. *Journal of Educational Psychology, 83*(1), 73–87. doi:10.1037/0022-0663.83.1.73

39. Wineburg, S. S. (2001). *Historical thinking and other unnatural acts: Charting the future of teaching the past.* Philadelphia, PA: Temple University Press.

Two

Teacher and Student Roles

Walking the Gradually Changing Line of Responsibility

Liwei Wei and P. Karen Murphy

How students think—indeed the extent to which they really need to think in school—and consequently what they can learn depend a lot on how their teachers respond to their students' responses.

Martin Nystrand (p. 29)[1]

Several years ago, fifth graders in one of our studies read and discussed a story about Satchel Paige. For those unfamiliar, Paige is considered one of the greatest baseball pitchers of all time. A predominant question explored by the students pertained to the importance of the role of the pitcher in baseball. There was some agreement that the leadership role taken on by the pitcher was particularly important in that the pitcher sets the tone for the team. A baseball team without a strong pitcher would always lose and the team motivation would decrease. One of the girls suggested that in fast-pitch softball a good pitcher who strikes the other team out makes the team look good, whereas a bad pitcher exposes her team's defensive weaknesses. Similarly, a poor defense puts additional pressure on the pitcher to control the opposing team at the plate and not allow any hits. In the end, all of the students seemed to agree that interactions between the pitcher and the other players influence the attitude and subsequent success of the team. The way in which the roles of the pitcher and other players impact the team's success is somewhat similar to the influence of the roles of teachers and students in classrooms.

In essence, the roles that teachers and students adopt fundamentally alter the nature of teaching and learning in classrooms. For example, these roles influence how teachers respond to their students; the ways knowledge is conceptualized and examined in the classroom; the development of students' critical-analytic thinking, reasoning, and beliefs about knowledge and knowing;[2] as well as what counts as success. Further, small-group discussions, especially those intended to foster high-quality talk, place additional demands on both teachers and students.[3] Indeed, teacher and student roles must shift from what might be pedagogically familiar or comfortable in whole-class instruction to less familiar, complex roles in order to foster quality talk in small groups. In this chapter, we highlight the importance of teacher and student roles in fostering student talk and delineate specific teacher roles and student roles that are essential to conducting high-quality, productive discussions in small groups.

In whole-class instruction where teachers employ a quiz-bowl approach, students acquire and affirm the belief that knowledge is a transmission of information from the teacher to the student. This type of instructional pattern is often referred to as an IRE model (e.g., Initiate-Respond-Evaluate) and is pervasive in classrooms around the world.[4] Teacher and student roles are essential in framing a given discussion approach. The key decisions that teachers make influence how the discussion will unfold. These decisions may include who selects the text to be discussed, who controls the topic of the discussion, who controls turn-taking during the discussion, who possesses the interpretive authority during the discussion,[5] and what types of pre- and post-discussion activities are desired. In the aforementioned IRE whole-class instruction, when teachers ask questions and praise answers predetermined by an authority, they are holding and exerting complete interpretative authority over the text or content. In these classrooms, teachers control most of the instructional and procedural choices, from the choice of the text to student turn-taking (e.g., calling on students when it is their turn to talk).

Unfortunately, when teachers maintain complete control over the discussion by frequently interjecting comments into the conversation and correcting students' responses, student participation will decrease and eventually fade from the discussion with the belief that teachers are the only source of knowledge. Such discussions are not only less productive, but they give way to lower cognitive effort and engagement by students. Further, in the IRE classroom, when teachers act as the quiz-bowl director, students are more likely to be exposed to questions that assess memorization of predetermined answers; what we refer to as test questions. As a result, students in those classrooms may be able to recall the answers to those specific questions, but they would be less prepared to answer questions requiring interpretation or synthesis of information. Moreover, it is difficult for these students to think critically or analytically about, around, and with text and content, because they have not been provided with instruction or space to practice such skills.

High-quality discussions, by comparison, require a very different approach to teaching and learning. Such discussions require teachers to serve a variety of roles, including intentional instructor, fading facilitator, and effortful evaluator. Students' roles change as well. A student must become an engaged learner, a thoughtful interpreter, and a reflexive responder. These roles are interdependent and, in concert, lead to discussions in which teachers' actions and discourse serve to facilitate students' use of talk as a tool for thinking and interthinking.[6] In essence, as students talk with each other, they are exposed to the discourse generated by others, and thus their thinking is interwoven and transformed. The aim is for the talk that occurs in a public setting to ultimately become internalized by the student as an outcome of their individual learning.[7]

In sum, we know that teacher and student roles have a dramatic impact on the nature and quality of classroom discussions. The purpose of this chapter is to explore teacher and student roles that support quality talk in classrooms, resulting in the enhancement of students' critical thinking and reasoning. Following our exploration of the various roles, we also forward practical guidance for practitioners who may aspire to employ high-quality discussions in their classrooms.

TEACHER ROLES

A teacher plays multiple, complex roles in productive, small-group discussions. In productive discussions, she must at times serve as an instructor, other times as a facilitator, as well as a feedback provider. Moreover, teachers must know when to shift within and among these roles or when to enact multiple roles simultaneously. In the subsequent sections, we explore the various roles of teachers in small-group discussions and provide discourse examples extracted from a fourth-grade language arts classroom.

Teacher as Intentional Instructor

Productive talk does not occur naturally or spontaneously in classrooms. Rather, productive talk must be cultivated. Indeed, when most teachers attended school they were acculturated into an IRE model of teaching; instruction based on the IRE model is quite familiar to them. Further, even students in primary school have experienced years of education where the primary roles of the teacher were knowledge teller and knowledge quizzer, whereas the students played the roles of passive absorber and polite responder. To combat such ingrained expectations of the roles of teachers and students, effective use of talk in a classroom must be explicitly taught, both to teachers and to students.

Though teachers can procure an understanding of productive talk through professional development, it is also necessary that they alter their instruction accordingly. In the absence of explicit instruction and scaffolded support and reinforcement, students will likely maintain their current participatory model—that is, in the absence of intentional instruction on productive talk, students are less likely to produce the ideal discourse elements (e.g., authentic questions, elaborated explanations, or exploratory talk) that signify high-quality talk.[8,9] The upshot, however, is that students can be taught about productive discussions and the roles they play in such discourse. As such, it is suggested that teachers play the role of an intentional instructor to provide explicit instruction for students on the discourse elements essential to high-quality discussions. This type of instruction solidifies the key elements of effective talk in the mind of the teacher while simultaneously offering an opportunity for students to come to know and practice effective tools for discussion.

According to Soter and her colleagues, the specific discourse elements that serve as indicators of productive talk include open-ended or authentic questions, uptake questions, elaborated explanation, and exploratory talk.[9] Specifically, open-ended or authentic questions can elicit more elaborated and extended responses. This type of questioning is in direct opposition to the low-level, declarative questioning where students are meant to parrot a simple, factual response to test-like questions, similar to that of the earlier IRE example. Uptake is a question that quite literally "takes up" a point or issue or question that someone else has said or asked, which indicates students' engagement with each other's ideas as well as students' co-construction of knowledge.[1,9] In terms of responses, an elaborated explanation "encourages explainers to clarify and reorganize the material in their own minds to make it understandable to others and, in the process, helps them develop new perspectives and recognize and fill in gaps in their understanding" (p. 13).[10,11] Exploratory talk involves students challenging each other's arguments.[12,13] In response to the challenge, students may rebut and explain why the challenge is not valid. In other cases, students may adjust their initial responses and refine their understanding based on the challenge.

Taken together, when teachers intentionally instruct students how to ask questions that elicit elaborated responses and how to answer questions with valid reasons and evidence, students are more likely to initiate these discourse elements during the discussion, particularly if these activities are modeled and reinforced by the teacher. The explicit instruction may take place in the form of mini-lessons that are delivered across an instructional sequence such that students learn about one discourse element at a time with corresponding opportunities to practice using that discourse element before learning the next one. It is important to note, however, that explicit instruction alone may not be sufficient; explicit instruction should be paired with modeling of the discourse elements by the teacher and guided practices, which allow students to engage in the use of the discourse element in pairs or small groups. This type of intentional instruction and guided practice can prepare students to more effectively apply the critical questioning and argumentation skills in conducting quality discussions.[14,15,16]

As an intentional instructor, teachers can also structure pre-discussion and post-discussion activities to further increase the impact of small-group discussions. Indeed, in addition to the skills needed to yield quality talk during the discussion, effective pre-discussion activities can prepare students for a productive discussion and set the discussion in motion.[17] Specifically, pre-discussion activities should activate students' prior knowledge about the topic and ready connections students can make to the current text. As mentioned in Chapter 1, this type of preparation helps students build a situation model. The purpose of post-discussion activities, on the other hand, is to support the transfer of students' comprehension skills demonstrated in the oral discourse to other domains or tasks such as essay writing or argumentative writing.[18] Essentially, post-discussion activities afford students an opportunity to reorganize and solidify the content learned in the discussion while also transferring it to new contexts.

Teacher as Fading Facilitator

Perhaps the most important aspect of teachers' roles is that they transition from the role of an overt instructor to that of a facilitator. Though the teacher's behavior is still intentional and purposeful, as she takes on the role of a fading facilitator, she shares control over turns and topic with students while gradually releasing more responsibility to students over time.

As articulated in Chapter 1, the specific stance that is espoused influences the extent to which teachers share control with students.[5] In expressive discussions, teachers exert less control over turns and topic than in efferent discussions, and in critical-analytic discussions teachers and students share control. In addition to the requirements of the espoused stance, like any other academic task, teachers take a primary role at the beginning (e.g., instructing or modeling) but gradually release responsibility to the students through purposeful fading as the discourse skills of the group mature.[19] As a facilitator, teachers use discourse moves (e.g., modeling, prompting, or challenging) to guide students toward engaging in productive talk. At the same time, teachers also use discourse moves (e.g., procedural) to maintain the flow of the discussion and ensure participation from all members of the group. As the more knowledgeable other in the group, teachers scaffold students within their zone of proximal development such that students' potential can be developed.[7,20] Gradually, as teachers continue to use purposeful teacher moves, students begin to acculturate the practices of the teacher, adjust their roles in a small-group discussion, and become familiar with the climate and normative expectations of small-group discussions. The teacher can then decreasingly fade from the discussion and still achieve their discourse goals for the group, while the students begin to engage in an open participation style of discourse. Eventually, students are expected to take on complete interpretative and procedural authority and be capable of conducting high-quality discussions independently. Indeed, it is often when students extensively hold the floor that quality talk emerges from the discussions.[9]

Unfortunately, the transition from a teacher-centered classroom to an open participation discourse structure is not easy. Specifically, teachers may wrestle with determining the best course of action to ensure students' participation and conceptual understanding.[21] The course of action becomes even more challenging as teachers release increasing responsibility to students (i.e., teachers have less control over the discussion). Although key to enhancing students' critical-analytic thinking, an open participation structure of discourse is not without its challenges, as various problems that hinder the outcome of the discussion may occur. For instance, some students may be too shy to speak whereas others may dominate the conversation. Alternatively, some students may make off-topic comments or express misconceptions during the small-group discussion. Indeed, despite the release in responsibility during the small-group discussion, teachers still exert a tremendous impact on student talk and the outcome of the discussion by addressing the aforementioned challenges, even if the proportion of teacher talk to student talk is low.[22] As the facilitator of small-group discussions, it is the role of the teacher to direct her attention to what is being said, how it is being said, and by whom, simultaneously.[3] In other words, during a discussion, teachers closely observe student discourse and respond to them using teacher discourse moves to promote productive talk.

In response, Wei, Murphy, and Firetto forwarded an integrated Teacher Move Taxonomy (TMT; see Table 2.1) to inform practitioners about available teacher discourse moves.[23] This taxonomy serves as a handy guide for teachers to refer to when they need to address challenging situations in their small-group discussions. Notably, the 12 teacher discourse moves included in the TMT were identified through a systematic literature review and iterative refinement through a series of card sorting and coding activities. Further, the 12 teacher discourse moves are common to discussion approaches identified as effective in promoting reading comprehension.

Table 2.1 Teacher Move Taxonomy (TMT)

Type	Definition	Example Quote
Back channeling	The teacher indicates that she/he is listening to the student within a few words (e.g., OK, yeah, and alright).	"OK." "Alright." "Yeah." "Uh-huh."
Challenging	The teacher challenges a student to consider an alternative point of view.	"Does that prove she was nice to them though?"
Checking	The teacher tries to make sure that every student has a basic literal understanding of the text.	"So, now, did the people on the Pony Express, did they go the whole route?"

Type	Definition	Example Quote
Clarifying	The teacher prompts a student to provide a clearer response by asking a question that sometimes includes a teacher's refined version of the student's response.	"So you think that— you're talking about when this took place?"
Debriefing	The teacher gives summarized comments on students' performance usually at the end of a group discussion.	"Good. So I think we had a good discussion today. I think everyone, um, participated. I think everyone—we're doing a great job of not raising your hand."
Instructing	The teacher gives explicit instructions on background knowledge, content of the text, and discussion-related skills or rules.	"Remember, we're talking to each other and not—like, we're not just talking to me, OK?"
Marking	The teacher draws attention to or reinforces specific aspects of a student's discourse by explicitly pointing it out.	"That was great— bringing up another text that we've all read about."
Modeling	The teacher exhibits an aspect of discourse that she/ he would like students to make by explicitly stating what she/he is going to do.	"So, let me ask a follow up question."
Procedural	The teacher manages the flow and directs the focus of the discussion.	"Let's move onto a new topic, because we're getting away from the text, OK?"

(Continued)

Table 2.1 (Continued)

Type	Definition	Example Quote
Prompting	The teacher helps a student construct an elaborate response. For example, sometimes the teacher may ask for reasons and evidence from the students.	"So why do we think that? Can we think of any evidence from the text?"
Reading	The teacher reads the text aloud to the students as a read-aloud activity or as a reference to the text for information during the discussion.	"I'd like to ask you a question about, on page 444, it says, 'After Paul and Babe settled on the river, they—and spent the day rolling the logs down the river, and he was so tired, he said . . .'"
Summarizing	The teacher overviews a part of the discussion thus helping build coherence for students.	"So I think we're—we've come to the conclusion that this story took place, you know, in the past, not in the present, and that it takes place in the South, but in the United States."

As we conclude this section on the role of a fading facilitator, we offer several exemplars of teachers from our own research who used teacher moves identified in the TMT to address challenges they were facing in small-group discussions. In the first example, when students were not providing elaborated responses, the teacher used *prompting* to encourage justification using reasons or evidence. Specifically, she prompted students by saying, "So why do we think that? Can we think of any evidence from the text?" In the second example, a fourth-grade language arts teacher used *challenging* to help a student reconstruct his understanding when the student provided a piece of evidence that did not support the claim. In the discussion, one student was talking about Adelina and her family being nice to the whales that entered the bay. When students were prompted by the teacher to provide evidence in support of the claim (i.e., Adelina and her family were nice to the whales), another student selected a piece of information in the text that says Adelina always went to see the whales. As opposed to pointing out that the student's response was incorrect or immediately *posing* the "correct answer," the teacher challenged the student with a question, "Does that prove she was nice to them though?" The excerpt from the discussion where the teacher used the discourse move of challenging to point out a possible illogical explanation in a student's response is shown in Figure 2.1.

In response to the teacher's discourse move, students in the discussion group are given an opportunity to reflect on their initial explanation, consider alternatives, and, potentially, reorganize their responses. As evidenced in previous research, effective teacher discourse moves can influence student talk and thinking.[22,24] Specifically, when the teacher prompts for evidence or relational thinking, it is more likely that students will respond with evidence and generate desired thinking in the following turns.

Teacher as Effortful Evaluator

The last of the teacher roles is that of an effortful evaluator. In the traditional IRE model, evaluation focuses primarily on students providing the expected or "correct" response. However,

Text: *Adelina's Whales*		
Turn	Speaker	Transcribed Talk
1.	Noah	I think the whales are close to the humans because like how other humans, when they don't really like animals, they kind of try to get them away and like harass them. But Adelina's family and grandfather always are like nice to them. That's probably why the whales were close to them. Cuz they were nice to them.
2.	Miss Garcia	How do you know they were nice to them? Can you find some evidence from the story that tells us they were nice to them?
3.	Lee	Well, Adelina always wanted to... always after school... she always ran to the ocean and wanted to hear the whales talk... to see them.
4.	Miss Garcia	Does that prove she was nice to them though?
5.	Lee	Sort of.
6.	Miss Garcia	It's because she LIKES them.
7.	Mia	It's because she likes the sound and what they do, but it doesn't prove that she's nice to them.

Figure 2.1 Excerpt from a fourth-grade classroom discussion on *Adelina's Whales*

when teachers facilitate small-group discussions, the role of an evaluator requires substantially more effort. Teachers must concentrate on listening to the student talk as it unfolds during the discussion in order to gauge students' high-level comprehension. Thus, serving as an evaluator is not only hard work but also requires a great deal of effortful cognitive energy and capacity on the part of the teacher. As teachers serve in the role of an effortful evaluator, they must listen carefully to students' talk to see if: (a) students are asking authentic questions, (b) students' responses are supported with reasons and evidence, and (c) students' conceptual understanding of the text or content is normatively appropriate (e.g., accurate or comprehensive). Based on these informal evaluations, teachers can determine whether to provide formative or summative feedback. Indeed, extensive, empirical education research has consistently found that feedback through appropriate teacher scaffolding is essential for enhancing students' learning and achievement.[25]

First, teachers may provide formative feedback during the discussion as they assess students' talk to fine-tune the discussion in real time. Recall that talk is an externalization of students' cognitive processes during the discussion, so student talk is, consequently, evidence of their comprehension or understanding of the content. Indeed, when students use talk for thinking critically and analytically together with their group members, their discourse during the discussion becomes an indicator of their thinking.[5,6,7] As emphasized earlier with respect to teachers' instructor role, certain discourse indicators in student talk are indicative of their critical and analytic thinking.[9] For instance, a student who offers an elaborated explanation with a claim, a reason, and corresponding evidence or an episode of talk where a student brings up a challenge are both considered important signs of critical and analytic thinking.[26,27] When teachers serve as an effortful evaluator, part of this role includes gauging the quality of the talk in situ and providing the requisite feedback to further enhance students' learning.

In addition, teachers can provide summative feedback immediately after the discussion. When providing summative feedback, teachers can suggest future goals to help students focus on the aspects of the discussion that can be attained within their zone of proximal development. As an example, a teacher may make it a goal for students to each ask one of the prepared authentic questions. The goals may address students' use of discourse elements (e.g., provide at least two reasons for every claim, or challenge other group members more often) as well as discussion goals in general (e.g., invite others to speak, or don't interrupt while others are talking).

The primary challenge with respect to the effortful evaluator role is: How can teachers effectively provide feedback without taking the interpretative authority from students? Essentially, how can the seemingly conflicting roles of effortful evaluator and fading facilitator be resolved? Herein, we offer several exemplars of teachers from our own research who used teacher moves to balance their roles as an effortful evaluator and a fading facilitator. According to the TMT, instructing, marking, and debriefing are potentially effective teacher moves for providing feedback during and after the discussion.[23] For instance, teachers may give brief instruction during the discussion as formative feedback. As a case in point, one of the teachers from our research used an *instructing* move to provide formative feedback by reminding students about one of the discussion rules, "Remember, we're talking to each other and not—like, we're not just talking to me, OK?" On the other hand, when teachers want to reinforce desirable student discourse, they may use a *marking* move as formative feedback to encourage other group members to generate similar discourse elements. One of the teachers helping us think more deeply about discussion engaged in marking when she said, "That was great—bringing up another text that we've all read about." That was a particularly effective marking move, as the teacher explicitly and specifically pointed out which aspect of the discourse was being marked (i.e., the generation of a cross text connection) rather than just offering generic praise (e.g., "good job!"). Explicit marking moves can help students get a clearer idea about the type of talk they should be using within the discussions. Indeed, as suggested by Lin and colleagues, teachers' explicit praise of students' use of evidence increased the likelihood of growth in student thinking.[22] Similarly, when teachers provide summative feedback immediately following the discussion, they may use a *debriefing* move to comment on students' performance in the discussion and set goals for future discussions. In our work in schools, an excerpt of a debriefing move used by one of the teachers was, "Good. So I think we had a good discussion today. I think everyone, um, participated. I think everyone—we're doing a great job of not raising your hand." In this way, teachers do not seem to take away students' interpretative authority or interrupt the flow of the discussion yet teachers successfully reinforce the desired student behaviors that contribute to a productive discussion.

Guidance for Practitioners

- Devote blocks of time to explicit instruction and guided practice for students on how to ask questions and construct responses that promote productive discussions.
- Provide instructional support before the discussion, such as individual or dyad practice generating questions, and after the discussion through writing tasks related to the discussion.
- Use small-group discussions as an instructional tool for enabling students to gain interpretive authority and to co-construct knowledge with their peers.
- Reconceptualize the evaluation of discussions by including the process of the discussion (i.e., students' ability to ask questions, provide elaborated responses, and respond to their peers) alongside content knowledge. Provide formative and summative feedback during and after the discussion.

STUDENT ROLES

Just as teachers have specified roles in effective discussions, so, too, do students—roles that align with or are responsive to the roles of the teacher. When a teacher plays the role of an intentional instructor, students are required to complete assigned tasks in preparation for their group discussions (i.e., as an engaged learner). When a teacher plays the role of a fading facilitator, it is expected that students take on more interpretative authority and control over the discussion, thus obtaining ownership of their knowledge (i.e., as a thoughtful interpreter). Finally, when a teacher serves as an effortful evaluator and gives feedback regarding students' discourse, students may take the opportunity to reflect on that feedback and modify their talk accordingly (i.e., as a reflexive responder).

Student as Engaged Learner

In high-quality discussions, students are engaged in their own learning. Students equip themselves with the requisite discussion skills and learn about the normative expectations of discussion like turn-taking. These discussion skills and rules can be acquired from the intentional instructor's mini-lessons and accompanying guided practice. As addressed previously, students must learn the discourse tools that promote high-level comprehension. These discourse tools include various types of authentic questions that involve deductive reasoning, inductive reasoning, speculative thinking, as well as questions that invite connections made to other texts, personal experience, or shared knowledge.[9] In addition, students must also learn to generate responses that incorporate multiple reasons or evidence and exploratory talk that involves the use of challenge over multiple turns. What is clear is that students who produce more elaborated explanations during the discussion learned more than those with unelaborated responses.[26] In sum, students must engage in the discussions by generating authentic questions and responding to questions using reasons and evidence. This type of engaged learning, although cognitively difficult, will pay dividends in terms of students' high-level comprehension and content-area understandings.

Further, as students gear up for the discussion, they should prepare questions to talk about and activate their prior knowledge about the text and the content to be discussed. Specifically, students may engage in pre-discussion activities such as writing various types of authentic, open-ended questions. Another type of pre-discussion exercise would be for students to respond to questions that elicit their general prior knowledge as well as topic-specific knowledge related to the text, such as "What do I know about the text or the topic?" Students' completion of these activities plays an important role in engaging their basic comprehension of the text and providing a solid foundation for the discussion.

Student as Thoughtful Interpreter

Over a series of discussions, students begin to take on increasing responsibility for conducting effective discussions, which necessarily requires increased student talk as well as critical-analytic thinking. Indeed, a student's role of thoughtful interpreter complements that of the fading facilitator—as teachers decreasingly fade their role, concomitant changes are seen as students take on that responsibility. Essentially, students take on the role of a thoughtful interpreter of the text and content as well as the talk within the group by initiating authentic questions, providing well-reasoned responses, and examining each other's arguments.

In this more teacher-like role, students become the interpreters of the content and discourse by examining their own thinking and that of their peers in relation to the text and the content. Indeed, instead of waiting for the teacher to explore some aspect of the text or to explain a scientific phenomenon or concept, students are able to actively construct their interpretation of the reading and associated discourse, and therefore regard themselves as a source of knowledge. Importantly, when students ask and respond to questions with genuine interest and engagement, it is more likely that their critical-analytic thinking will be stimulated and spread among other members within the discussion group.[1,9,27,28,29] In addition, students who take on interpretative authority are more likely to address the questions and respond to their group members, as opposed to deferring to the teacher as the authority.[30]

Necessarily, thoughtful interpretation requires that students practice taking on interpretative authority, while actively and carefully considering and engaging with multiple perspectives, including their own questions and responses during the discussion. Therefore, high-quality discussions require students to capitalize on what they learn from the mini-lessons and use the critical-analytic thinking skills and discussion rules as students serve in the role of a thoughtful interpreter of the talk, text, and content.

Student as Reflexive Responder

A key feature of participation within a discussion is that of listening and responding. When students participate in small-group discussions, they are exposed to a wide array of discourse sequences from other students and the teacher. As such, students have the opportunity to appropriate others' discourse moves as they become more comfortable with the nature of productive talk. As a case in point, studies show that the use of argument stratagems snowballs among students in the discussion group over time,[28] and that students are more likely to model their peers' relational thinking strategy.[22] In the same way, students also begin to spontaneously generate teacher discourse moves such as prompting and praising their peers for using evidence.[24]

Indeed, during small-group discussions, students learn and reflect on the discourse generated by their peers and the teacher to enhance high-level comprehension both individually and as a group. As is the case when students learn by listening to their fellow classmates, they can also utilize teacher feedback in ways that foster and enhance high-level comprehension. Indeed, as reflexive responders, students also can make valuable use of teachers' formative and summative feedback during and after the discussion. It is not just that students become better at asking and responding to questions, but also that they are able to guide themselves and their peers toward deeper text and content understandings by reflecting on the discourse of the group and the feedback of the teacher. In the same way that Lev Vygotsky asserted that learning occurs in the public first and then becomes internalized within the individual,[7] so it is that a reflexive responder internalizes the group discourse and teacher feedback for later individual use.

Guidance for Practitioners

- Empower students to conduct productive discussions by activating their prior knowledge about the text and content, providing them with opportunities to generate questions in preparation for the discussion, and reviewing expectations in discussion behaviors.
- Avoid the tendency to provide immediate corrections, redirection, or explanations in order to allow students to engage as thoughtful interpreters.
- Explicitly and intentionally model, mark, and direct students' attention toward the discourse moves that they need to adopt in order to conduct effective discussions such that students can internalize these discourse moves for individual growth.

CODA

Taken together, small-group discussions that promote students' high-level comprehension require multifaceted teacher and student roles. As delineated throughout the chapter, teacher and student roles have a tremendous impact on the outcomes of small-group discussion and determine the extent to which students enhance their high-level comprehension. However, like the roles of various players on a baseball or softball team, these roles are not static, nor are they independent of each other—teachers' and students' roles are interdependent and change over time.

Teachers provide explicit instructions with guided practice, gradually release interpretative authority and responsibility to students, as well as give students formative and summative feedback. Concomitantly, students learn about the essential discourse elements and interpret the text and the content while learning to use discourse moves from their peers and teachers. As these skills and abilities are honed, the various roles of those within the discussion shift, just as pitchers and fielders adjust to each other. Whereas the pitcher may have begun as the most valuable player, his role and importance diminishes as the defensive players improve and take on more of the defensive burden. In this same light, over time, the central importance of the teacher diminishes as the student's responsibility and interpretive authority is cultivated and begins to flourish. No doubt, facilitating small-group discussions is a delicate skill that requires teachers to know what type of discourse move is desired and when it should be used.[31] By harnessing the power of different types of teacher discourse moves, teachers can better guide students toward critical and analytic thinking within their zone of proximal development. Ultimately, however, the goal in high-quality discussions is for the teacher and students to mutually contribute to meaningful learning through rich, critical-analytic discourse.

REFERENCES

1. Nystrand, M. (with Gamoran, A., Kachur, R., & Prendergast, C.). (1997). *Opening dialogue: Understanding the dynamics of language and learning in the English classroom.* New York, NY: Teachers College Press.

2. Hofer, B. K. (2002). Personal epistemology as a psychological and educational construct: An introduction. In B. K. Hofer & P. R. Pintrich (Eds.), *Personal epistemology: The psychology of beliefs about knowledge and knowing* (pp. 3–14). Mahwah, NJ: Erlbaum.

3. Gall, M. D., & Gall, J. P. (1993). *Teacher and student roles in different types of classroom discussions.* Paper presented at the annual meeting of American Educational Research Association, Atlanta, GA.

4. Mehan, H. (1979). *Learning lessons: Social organization in the classroom.* Cambridge, MA: Harvard University Press.

5. Chinn, C. A., Anderson, R. C., & Waggoner, M. A. (2001). Patterns of discourse in two kinds of literature discussion. *Reading Research Quarterly, 36,* 378–411. doi:10.1598/rrq.36.4.3

6. Mercer, N. (2000). *Words and minds: How we use language to think together.* London, UK: Routledge.

7. Vygotsky, L. S. (1978). *Mind in society: The development of higher mental psychological processes.* Cambridge, MA: Harvard University Press.

8. Li, M., Murphy, P. K., Wang, J., Mason, L. H., Firetto, C. M., Wei, L., & Chung, K.-S. (2016). Promoting reading comprehension and critical-analytic thinking: A comparison of three approaches with fourth and fifth graders. *Contemporary Educational Psychology, 46,* 101–115. doi:10.1016/j. cedpsych.2016.05.002

9. Soter, A. O., Wilkinson, I. A. G., Murphy, P. K., Rudge, L., Reninger, K., & Edwards, M. (2008). What the discourse tells us: Talk and indicators of high-level comprehension. *International Journal of Educational Research, 47,* 372–391. doi:10.1016/j.ijer.2009.01.001

10. Webb, N. M., Farivar, S. H., & Mastergeorge, A. M. (2002). Productive helping in cooperative groups. *Theory into Practice, 41*(1), 13–20. doi:10.1207/s15430421tip4101_3

11. Bargh, J. A., & Schul, Y. (1980). On the cognitive benefit of teaching. *Journal of Educational Psychology, 72,* 593–604.

12. Barnes, D. (1976). *From communication to curriculum.* Harmondsworth, UK: Penguin Books.

13. Mercer, N. (2002). Developing dialogues. In G. Wells & G. Claxton (Eds.), *Learning for life in the 21st century: Sociocultural perspectives on the future of education* (pp. 141–153). Oxford, UK: Blackwell.

14. Mercer, N., Dawes, L., Wegerif, R., & Sams, C. (2004). Reasoning as a scientist: Ways of helping children to use language to learn science. *British Educational Research Journal, 30,* 359–378. doi:10.1080/01411920410001689689

15. RAND Reading Study Group. (2002). *Reading for understanding: Toward an R&D program in reading comprehension.* Santa Monica, CA: RAND.

16. Rosenshine, B., Meister, C., & Chapman, S. (1996). Teaching students to generate questions: A review of the intervention studies. *Review of Educational Research, 66,* 181–221. doi:10.2307/1170607

17. Murphy, P. K., Firetto, C. M., Wei, L., Li, M., & Croninger, R. M. V. (2016). What really works: Optimizing classroom discussions to promote comprehension and critical-analytic thinking. *Policy Insights from the Behavioral and Brain Sciences*, 3(1), 27–35. doi:10.1177/2372732215624215

18. Chesser, W. D., Gellalty, G. B., & Hale, M. S. (1997). Do Paideia Seminars explain higher writing scores? *Middle School Journal*, 29, 40–44. doi:10.1080/00940771.1997.11494485

19. Pearson, P. D., & Gallagher, M. C. (1983). The instruction of reading comprehension. *Contemporary Educational Psychology*, 8, 20–22.

20. Wood, D. J., Bruner, J. S., & Ross, G. (1976). The role of tutoring in problem solving. *Journal of Child Psychiatry and Psychology*, 17(2), 89–100. doi:10.1111/j.1469-7610.1976.tb00381.x

21. Murphy, P. K., Greene, J. A., & Firetto, C. M. (2014). *Quality Talk: Developing students' discourse to promote critical-analytic thinking, epistemic cognition, and high-level comprehension.* (Technical Report No. 1). University Park: The Pennsylvania State University.

22. Lin, T. J., Jadallah, M., Anderson, R. C., Baker, A. R., Nguyen-Jahiel, K., Kim, I.-H., . . . Wu, X. (2015). Less is more: Teachers' influence during peer collaboration. *Journal of Educational Psychology*, 107, 609–629. doi:10.1037/a0037758

23. Wei, L., Murphy, P. K., & Firetto, C. M. (2016, April). *Toward an integrated taxonomy of teacher discourse moves in small-group text-based discussions.* Roundtable presented at the annual meeting of the American Educational Research Association, Washington, DC.

24. Jadallah, M., Anderson, R. C., Nguyen-Jahiel, K., Miller, B., Kim, I.-H., Kuo, L., . . . Wu, X. (2011). Influence of a teacher's scaffolding moves during child-led small-group discussions. *American Educational Research Journal*, 48, 194–230. doi:10.3102/0002831210371498

25. Hattie, J., & Timperley, H. (2007). The power of feedback. *Review of Educational Research*, 77, 81–112. doi:10.3102/003465430298487

26. Chinn, C. A., O'Donnell, A. M., & Jinks, T. S. (2000). The structure of discourse in collaborative learning. *Journal of Experimental Education*, 69, 77–97. doi:10.1080/00220970009600650

27. Webb, N. M. (1989). Peer interaction and learning in small groups. *International Journal of Educational Research*, 13, 21–39. doi:10.1016/0883-0355(89)90014-1

28. Anderson, R. C., Nguyen-Jahiel, K., McNurlen, B., Archodidou, A., Kim, S., Reznitskaya, A., . . . Gilbert, L. (2001). The snowball phenomenon:

Spread of ways of talking and ways of thinking across groups of children. *Cognition and Instruction, 19*, 1–46. doi:10.1207/s1532690xci1901_1

29. Nystrand, M., Wu, L., Gamoran, A., Zeiser, S., & Long, D. (2003). Questions in time: Investigating the structure and dynamics of unfolding classroom discourse. *Discourse Processes, 35*, 135–198. doi:10.1207/s15326950dp3502_3

30. Anderson, R. C., Chinn, C., Chang, J., Waggoner, J., & Nguyen, K. (1998). Intellectually stimulating story discussions. In F. Osborn (Ed.), *Literacy for all: Issues in teaching and learning* (pp. 170–186). New York, NY: Guilford Press.

31. Hmelo-Silver, C. E. (2004). Problem-based learning: What and how do students learn. *Educational Psychology Review, 16*, 235–266. doi:10.1023/b:edpr.0000034022.16470.f3

Three

Pedagogical Decisions and Contextual Factors

Tipping the Scales Toward Highly Productive Discussions

Mengyi Li

The child begins to perceive the world not only through his eyes but also through his speech. As a result, the immediacy of "natural" perception is supplanted by a complex mediated process; as such, speech becomes an essential part of the child's cognitive development.

Lev Vygotsky (p. 32)[1]

Listening to a highly effective discussion is like listening to a jazz tune, where the saxophone, trumpet, and drum all contribute uniquely to a harmonious blend of music. Jazz music is known for its improvisation—a state in which musicians spontaneously create fresh melodies based on an original tune. As jazz musicians improvise, they alternate playing solos, continually building on each other to create great music that is both inventive and unique. This notion of jazz serves as an effective metaphor for high-quality discussions. Like jazz, high-quality discussions include the blending of different voices from varied cultural, ethnic, and academic backgrounds. Each student comes to the discussion having an understanding of the text to be discussed, yet each one brings her own unique prior knowledge and experiences. Throughout the discussion, the members listen actively to each other, provide feedback, share their own perspectives, and co-construct meaning as a group. Importantly, the composition of the jazz ensemble, like that of the discussion, necessarily impacts the resulting music that is produced. A group of ten musicians will produce an entirely different tune than a quartet; likewise, the number of students in a discussion will alter the resulting talk. Thus, in order to ensure discussions are filled with high-quality talk there are various contextual factors that teachers must consider as they make pedagogical decisions.

As one might suspect and as has been alluded to in previous chapters, not all discussions are equally effective.[2] Some discussion approaches like those that advocate a critical-analytic stance are more powerful than others at enhancing high-level comprehension and critical-analytic thinking,[2] and specific teacher and student roles are delineated so as to foster quality discussions. In the end, the quality of discussion also greatly influences the achievement of desirable learning outcomes. Essentially, the first two chapters of this volume provided a blueprint for high-quality discussions. However, as one would expect, even with a blueprint there are numerous factors in real-life settings that could influence the effects of those discussions. When implementing discussions in authentic classrooms, an array of contextual factors such as group type (e.g., size and composition), learner characteristics (e.g., ability, gender, or prior knowledge), and text features (e.g., genre, structure, or topic) impact the functioning and productivity of discussion.[3] Further, these factors may also dynamically interplay with each other in any given situation. The purpose of this chapter is to review findings from the extant literature on classroom discussion and to explore the factors that influence the building of a rich and meaningful discussion. Having explored various contextual factors for promoting quality discussions, the chapter concludes by forwarding several recommendations for practitioners.

GROUPING FACTORS

As jazz bands vary in the quantity of musicians and composition of instruments played by its members, discussion groups also vary in key grouping factors such as size and ability composition. With discourse, what is *optimal* may vary according to the focus of the discussion. Because our goal is to promote discussions that effectively foster high-level comprehension and critical-analytic thinking, we review empirical studies on the influence of grouping factors in the subsequent sections. In addition, this research is accompanied by authentic discourse examples collected from elementary school classrooms to allow the readers an idea of what such discourse *sounds like*.

Group Size

The first pedagogical decision that a teacher will likely consider before conducting a classroom discussion is whether to divide the class into small groups or keep them as a single, large group. An abundance of research over the past few decades has investigated the effects of within-class grouping on student discussion and learning.[4,5,6] A number of meta-analyses were conducted to compare the effects of small-group and whole-class settings and presented a fairly consistent picture regarding the superiority of small groups to whole-class instruction in fostering student interaction and learning outcomes.[7,8,9] Specifically, Lou and colleagues examined 51 empirical studies with students from first grade through college and compared the effects of grouping versus no grouping on student achievement.[8] Their results showed that within-class grouping positively influenced student learning in all content areas. Regardless of students' ability level (i.e., low, average, and high), they all benefited from being assigned to small groups. On average, low-achieving students gained statistically significantly more than the average-achieving students. They also found that the actual group size was strongly linked to grouping effect. The effect size for smaller groups with three to four members was statistically significantly larger than for groups with five to seven members.

Additionally, previous studies examining the effects of grouping on classroom discussions suggested that students' engagement, participation, and motivation were different in small-group settings than in whole-class settings. Webb and Kenderski examined the classroom interactions of junior high school students.[6] They recorded and coded student interactions for the classes working in small-group and whole-class settings separately. Interactions among students in the whole-class settings were infrequent; most occurred between teacher and student. Further, students specifically asked for help from the teacher instead of their peers. In contrast, students in small groups interacted more often with other students both by asking and providing explanations, which indicated that they engaged more actively in the co-construction of knowledge during discussions. Moreover, Theberge investigated students' classroom participation structures in a sixth-grade science class and discovered that turns were distributed more equitably among students in small-groups than in whole-class discussions.[10] In particular, girls contributed notably fewer turns than boys did in whole-class discussions. With respect to students' motivation, Wu and colleagues reported that students exhibited higher levels of interest and text engagement during peer-led small-group discussions than teacher-dominant whole-group discussions.[11] Similarly, Cao and Philp found that second language learners were less willing to communicate in whole-class settings than in small-group or dyad settings.[4] A majority of the studied participants attributed their relatively low participation in the whole-class settings to their lack of self-confidence in spoken English or their perceived inability to speak without prior planning.[12] Likewise, students who adopted more active speech roles in the whole-class setting reported being more self-confident than those who were less active. It is also well established in the literature that as group size increases both group cohesiveness and performance tend to decrease.[13] Here, group cohesiveness refers to "the resultant forces which are acting on the members to stay in a group" or simply group members' attraction toward the group (p. 274).[14] In a whole-class or other larger group setting, the lack of group cohesiveness may cause individual students to exert less effort to communicate or collaborate with other members and thus constrain the interactions necessary for a high-quality discussion.

To summarize, small-group discussions seem to be the optimal format for developing high-quality discussions. Findings from a number of meta-analyses provide converging evidence that students learn considerably better in small groups than in whole-class settings across subject areas, regardless of ability levels.[8] In small groups, students are more likely to obtain the control of turns, so they have more opportunities to engage in the discussion by sharing their thoughts publicly, giving and receiving elaborations, and co-constructing meaning with peers. "Shy" students, as well as second language learners who are not confident with their spoken English proficiency, may feel more secure talking in small-group settings. Smaller group size has also been linked to increased group cohesiveness, which drives students to stay committed to group goals and take on the responsibility to communicate and collaborate with peers.

Group Composition

Whereas the advantages of conducting small-group discussions are well established by previous findings, the next decision that a teacher may face is how to create small groups to facilitate effective, critical-analytic discussions. Though there appears to be no single best solution to this question, a notable consensus is that individual characteristics such as general academic achievement or subject-specific ability (e.g., reading fluency) should be taken into account when clustering students into small groups.[15] The most controversial issue underlying group composition is, however, whether students of similar ability levels should be placed together (i.e., homogeneous ability grouping) or students of different ability levels should be represented in each small group (i.e., heterogeneous ability grouping). The logic behind homogeneous grouping is that teachers can adapt their instructional pace to accommodate the special needs of particular groups (i.e., differentiated instruction).[16] For this reason, homogeneous grouping is often seen in tiered reading interventions.[17] Heterogeneous grouping, on the other hand, is encouraged by a majority of contemporary discussion approaches, as it takes advantage of student diversity and promotes collaboration and interdependence among peers.[18,19]

It is important to note, however, that the choice of group composition does influence the effectiveness of small-group discussions. The meta-analysis conducted by Lou and colleagues compared the effects of homogeneous ability grouping to heterogeneous ability grouping on student learning and reported that overall homogeneous ability grouping promotes better learning achievement.[8] However, the results are rather mixed when considering the impact of grouping composition at each of the different student ability levels. Essentially, low-achieving students are advantaged when they participate in heterogeneous ability groups, whereas average-achieving students learn better in homogeneous ability groups. In contrast, high-achieving students perform equally well in groups of either composition. Interestingly, subject area was found to moderate the effects of group composition on student learning. Students who participated in homogeneous ability groups had an advantage over heterogeneous ability groups with a medium effect size in the content areas of reading or language arts, but no significant differences were identified in math and science.

A number of individual studies also showed how group compositions affected the nature of the discussion, student interactions, and motivation.[15,20,21,22,23] For instance, Saleh and colleagues investigated fourth-grade students' classroom discussions in a biology course.[21] They found that low-ability students from heterogeneous ability groups were more optimistic about collaborating with peers to achieve a learning goal (i.e., collaborative learning) when compared to those from homogeneous ability groups. In line with the previously reviewed findings, the heterogeneously grouped low-ability students performed better on the subsequent achievement tests. In contrast, average- and high-ability students indicated higher motivation beliefs toward collaborative learning favoring homogeneous groups. Saleh and colleagues also compared student interactions and found that average-and high-ability students in homogeneous ability groups had higher ratios of collaborative elaboration than those in heterogeneous groups, as students of similar abilities tended to build upon each other's ideas when discussing with and reasoning about the lesson materials. Students in the heterogeneous ability groups generated higher proportions of individual elaborations (i.e., answering questions, resolving conflicts, and reasoning) than students in homogeneous ability groups, and without the higher achieving students in their groups, low-ability students in homogeneous ability groups neither gave nor benefitted from hearing elaborative responses. Specifically, in heterogeneous ability groups, low-ability students asked most of the questions while high-ability students raised few questions but provided most of the explanations. Of all ability levels, average-ability students contributed the least when engaged in heterogeneous ability group discussions.

A more recent study conducted by Murphy and colleagues explored the influence of homogeneous versus heterogeneous ability grouping on fourth- and fifth-grade students' text-based discussions in language arts classes.[15] Their research aligned with previous findings and showed that high-ability students were engaged and participated actively in both types of group composition by raising authentic questions, providing elaborated explanations, and reasoning about and around text. However, in contrast to previous findings, which suggested that low-ability students performed better in heterogeneous ability groups, Murphy and colleagues found that low-ability students asked fewer questions and their responses were often brief and less elaborated when in heterogeneous ability groups. Low-ability students tended to disengage in heterogeneous groups, where high-ability students often dominated the conversations, and thus low-ability students did not benefit as much from participating in the *talk*. In contrast, they found that low-ability students were quite engaged and active in homogeneous ability groups. However, with the absence of high-ability students, their discourse often digressed from the topic. Figure 3.1 shows a talk excerpt from a fourth-grade language arts class where five low-ability students discussed an expository text, *Smokejumpers*, from their basal readers.

In this example, Antonio identified a similarity between the selected text and animated movie that he and one other student in the group had previously watched. Though Antonio and Tom were both actively engaged in their conversation about the movie, their discourse quickly digressed and was only loosely related to the text. The teacher then intervened and tried to guide the discussion back to the focus of the text and reframed so that all students could participate.

Turn	Speaker	Transcribed Talk
		Text: *Smokejumpers*
1.	Antonio	And it also -- in *Planes: Fire & Rescue* -- they also tried to rescue the animal. Remember the deer that was way behind? In the --
2.	Tom	And then they go back.
3.	Antonio	-- yeah. And then, um, the, um, helicopter guy --
4.	Tom	Yeah.
5.	Antonio	-- picked them up with his hook, and he put them in front of the line.
6.	Mrs. Green	All right, kids.
7.	Tom	That was funny.
8.	Mrs. Green	You're having your own little discussion over here, Okay? So let's, let's um, move on to a new question not related to jumping out of an airplane.

Figure 3.1 Excerpt of discourse from a small-group discussion composed of five low-ability students in a homogeneous ability group

In sum, previous research reported mixed findings regarding the effects of group composition on classroom discussions in terms of student interaction, engagement, and motivation. Although homogeneous grouping seems to promote a higher proportion of collaborations among peers as well as better learning outcomes than heterogeneous grouping, the effects of group composition are different depending on students' ability levels. It seems that no singular form of group composition is optimal for all students. Heterogeneous grouping may be beneficial for low-achieving students, whereas homogeneous grouping may be advantageous for average-achieving students. Based on the findings reported here, teachers can be better informed about how within-class grouping influences the quality of discussions in order to make their pedagogical decisions accordingly. There are, of course, other contextual factors that need to be taken into account when determining a productive discussion, and those will be reviewed in the following sections.

Guidance for Practitioners

- Conduct classroom discussions in a small-group setting to stimulate effective, high-quality discourse. Small-group discussions are superior to whole-class discussions in terms of enhancing students' participation, engagement, and motivation.
- Match the content and learning goals with the unique aspects of the classroom as well as the needs of individual students to determine the best or most efficacious grouping scenario (i.e., homogeneous versus heterogeneous).

LEARNER CHARACTERISTICS

The aforementioned studies revealed how the decisions teachers make about group composition influence small-group discussions. However, irrespective of the composition of the groups, students' performance in group discussions is also shaped by a combination of their own characteristics and those of the groups.[25] As a result, it is imperative to also consider the characteristics of the learners and their influence on classroom discussions.

Ability

As reviewed previously, high-ability students perform equally well in homogeneous and heterogeneous groups.[8,21] The learning outcomes of these students seem to be unaffected by the group composition. However, there is evidence showing that their roles and discourse in small-group discussions are affected by group composition. High-ability students tend to dominate the conversations and may adopt the role of the teacher by providing more elaborated explanations to lower-ability group members.[23] In Figure 3.2, a heterogeneous group of five students is discussing an expository text, *Earth's Closest Neighbor*, from their basal reading series. The story mainly provides factual information about the moon and space.

Text: *Earth's Closest Neighbor*

Turn	Speaker	Transcribed Talk
1.	Michelle (low)	Why do you think that there's a dark side of the moon?
2.	Briana (high)	Because that's the side that's not facing the sun.
3.	Michelle (low)	Oh, right.
4.	Emma (high)	Well, the sun is when it's daytime, but then the moon comes when it's nighttime. So when the sun's facing us, it's the moon — on the dark side of the moon is facing somewhere else.
5.	Elijiah (average)	No, the dark side of the moon's facing towards us. The light side of the moon's facing the other way. That's what I hear.
6.	Briana (high)	Actually, um, it kinda um, actually, the moon always stays, and it doesn't turn [hand gesture]. Like, it basically goes around Earth but it doesn't spin in a circle.
7.	Michelle (low)	Yeah.
8.	Briana (high)	And so the light side of the moon and the dark side of the moon are always the same. Because there's always one side that's never — the light the moon gives reflects off the sun, so that's the side where there is no sun.

Figure 3.2 Excerpt of discourse from a small-group discussion composed of five students with varying ability levels

In the excerpt in Figure 3.2, a low-ability student (Michelle) raised a question that clearly required elaboration. The answer to the question was not specified in the discussed text, and it seemed that the low-ability student was genuinely interested in knowing the answer. After the question was posed, the two high-ability students (Briana and Emma) both answered the question by providing elaborations. While high-ability students extended their explanations, the two average-ability students were relatively quiet and reserved. One remained silent throughout the excerpt and the other only challenged the group when he felt there was a need to clarify errors. Meanwhile, the low-ability student only made brief confirmations, such as "Oh, right" and "Yeah," during the collaborative dialogue.

In essence, the discussion in Figure 3.2 exemplifies how high- and low-ability students often form a teacher-student relationship during group discussions composed of students with varying ability levels; low-ability students may exhibit help-seeking behaviors and receive help from the more capable students so as to fill in knowledge gaps and correct misconceptions.[20,22,26] As a result, high-ability students also develop more sophisticated reasoning skills by providing others with elaborated explanations.[27] A downside is that it leaves fewer opportunities for average-ability students to seek or receive help than what might be available in homogeneous groups.[25] Research also shows that average-ability students are less motivated about learning in heterogeneous groups.[28] Thus, teachers should be cognizant about this and provide necessary support to bolster average-ability students' engagement and participation during classroom discussions.

The teacher-student relationship is less commonly seen in homogeneous group discussions without the presence of low-ability students. Instead, high-ability students are found to produce more collaborative reasoning with other group members during homogeneous discussions.[24,29] Figure 3.3 is an excerpt of a discussion from a homogeneous group of high-ability students from a fourth-grade language arts class. Four high-ability students discussed a biographical text, *The Man Who Went to the Far Side of the Moon*, from their basal readers, which tells the story of the Apollo 11 astronaut, Michael Collins, who went to the moon but never got the chance to walk on its surface.

At the beginning of the discussion, Daniel raised a question attempting to make a connection between the discussed text and another text that they read two weeks ago, *Moonwalk*. In response to his question, the other group members each provided elaborative reasoning around and with the text by comparing and contrasting the two texts from different aspects (i.e., text and genre). Unlike the low-ability student in Figure 3.2 who asked and received elaborations rather passively, Daniel challenged as well

Text: *The Man Who Went to the Far Side of the Moon*

Turn	Speaker	Transcribed Talk
1.	Daniel	How is this story kinda like *Moonwalk*?
2.	Viera	Well, it's like *Moonwalk* because they're on the moon, and, um, there's two people on the moon. And they're different because, like, they're not brothers from what I know. They're not brothers.
3.	Daniel	Yeah, but they're really good friends.
4.	Evelyn	Yeah.
5.	Viera	This is nonfiction, and the other thing is fiction. And in this --
6.	Daniel	Science fiction.
7.	Viera	-- we don't have, yeah, we don't have enough evidence to say --
8.	Mia	(interrupting) Wait, wait, wait, wait, wait, wait... I think it's different because they were actually doing research on the moon and stuff, taking samples, but then Gerry and -- whatever his name is --
9.	Daniel	Verne.
10.	Mia	Gerry and Verne were jumping over rilles having fun until one of them got hurt and almost died.
11.	Viera	The thing is, they're just kids, and these people are experienced, they know what they're doing. The kids are kind of jumping around --
12.	Evelyn	The only thing...
13.	Viera	That's probably --
14.	Evelyn	The only thing that I find that's the same is that there's a bunch of facts in this one, but the other one was based on facts, there were some facts. But other than that they're completely different.
15.	Viera	Yeah.

Figure 3.3 Excerpt of discourse from a small-group discussion composed of four high-ability students in a homogeneous ability group

as collaborated with other group members to expand upon the discussion. Long periods of student talk were evident without teacher interruption, and the teacher clearly released responsibility and interpretive authority to students in this excerpt.

Similar to high-ability students, average-ability students were also more motivated to co-construct elaborations in homogeneous groups, which led to better learning outcomes.[21] Nevertheless, without the presence of higher-ability peers in homogenous groups, low-ability students gave and received fewer elaborations and were less likely to be exposed to the reasoning skills demonstrated by high achievers.[9] There was also higher likelihood that low-ability students would become inattentive in homogenous groups,[30] and even when they were engaged, their talk often digressed from the topic and required the teacher to guide them back to topic.[15]

Taken together, this section reviews the varied behavior and interaction patterns of students at different ability levels, accompanied by illustrative examples from authentic classroom discussions. No group composition is optimal for all students. Thus, when it comes to the assignment of students to discussion groups, teachers must match their content and learning goals with the needs of the students when determining the best or most efficacious grouping scenario. It is also worth noting that though heterogeneous groups may provide a greater benefit for lower-achieving students, they don't guarantee that students will receive the necessary conditions for success.[31] It is still critical for teachers to make prompt adjustments to ensure that all students engage in and benefit from classroom discussions (see Chapter 2 for more information).

Gender

In addition to ability, the gender of the students in the group also emerges as an important factor in the dynamic interactions of small-group discussions. A meta-analysis conducted by Leaper and Smith examined gender disparities in children's speech in classroom interactions and reported that female students were generally more talkative than male students.[32] Closer examinations of student talk and motivation suggested that girls were generally more motivated and engaged than boys in small-group discussions.[11] Moreover, girls were more likely to support and elaborate on others' talk, whereas boys often attempted to use more assertive speech to challenge others and establish power.[32] In small-group cooperative learning activities, girls were found to provide more elaborated answers in response to other students' questions.[33] In fact, Figure 3.3 provides a typical example of gender disparities that emerged in classroom discussions. That discussion group consisted of three females and one male. The male raised a question and the other three females actively responded to the question by generating connections to other texts. The male student made fewer elaborated responses and more often challenged or attempted to correct others (e.g., "but they're really good friends," "science fiction").

Unfortunately, when female students asked questions, their questions were more often neglected and less likely to obtain elaborated answers from other group members than those raised by male students.[34] It is possible that this finding is because female students asked more general questions that were difficult to answer, whereas male students asked more specific questions that were easier to respond to with elaborations. Regardless, overall the findings indicate that gender influences students' discussion engagement. Acknowledging these patterns is helpful for teachers to better promote high-quality discussions and subsequently enhance students' learning outcomes.

Other Learner Characteristics

Other learner characteristics such as prior knowledge and perceived interestingness have also been found to affect the quality of discussions. However, such research and the effects these characteristics have on small-group discussions have been sparse. Among the few studies that have considered these relationships, Goatley,

Brock, and Raphael explored the influence of prior knowledge and perceived interest by examining the discourse data from five students during small-group, text-based discussions over three weeks.[35] Their qualitative analyses suggested that the student who possessed the highest prior knowledge pertaining to the text topic tended to take a leading role in most of the discussions. The high-knowledge student initiated most of the questions, while other students seldom challenged her topic initiations. Other students would also like to attribute her as the more knowledgeable other and draw on her knowledge to construct meaning during discussions. Goatley and colleagues also noted that students' discussion engagement might have been influenced by students' interests triggered by text features (e.g., story events, characters' relationships, or illustrations). However, these effects were not quantitatively examined. A recent study conducted by Li investigated the effects of perceived interestingness on students' acquisition of high-level comprehension during small-group discussions and confirmed that perceived interest was a strong predictor of student engagement, as evidenced by their elaborated explanations generated in text-based discussions.[36]

In short, contemporary classrooms are often marked by the diversity of students. Teachers need to acknowledge the individual differences of students and adjust for their particular needs so as to enhance the quality of classroom discussion. For instance, it is recommended to evaluate students' prior knowledge before the discussion or the entire reading event and conduct pre-discussion activities accordingly to prime students' topic knowledge and better position them to benefit from the subsequent text-based discussions (see Chapter 5 for more information). The findings reviewed here are to provide teachers with a broad sense of how learner characteristics influence the dynamic processes of classroom discussions. More research is needed to further examine their effects on the quality of discussions.

Guidance for Practitioners

- Monitor students' performance in small-group discussions and employ appropriate teacher moves to ensure that students of all ability levels are actively engaged in productive talk.
- Acknowledge different gender roles in discussions, carefully using teacher moves to reduce gender disparity in students' discussion participation so as to enhance the quality of discussion.
- Embrace diversity in students' prior knowledge and interests to inspire student engagement in discussions.

TEXT FEATURES

When considering small-group, text-based discussions, the features of the text are of paramount importance, especially when the discussion goal is to achieve high-level comprehension of that text. Based on current literature on reading comprehension, text features such as text genre (e.g., narrative, expository, or mixed),[37] text structure (e.g., comparison, problem-and-solution, or cause-and-effect),[38] and text topic all play important roles in the resulting productivity of discussions. However, research in this area is rather limited.

Leal suggested that elementary school students were more engaged when discussing mixed genre texts like biographies than when discussing texts of other genres such as narrative or expository.[39] Yet, the discussion goal was not specified in this study and no achievement outcome was assessed. Another study conducted by Li, Murphy, and Firetto compared how narrative and expository texts influenced student talk in terms of high-level comprehension during small-group text-based discussions in fourth- and fifth-grade classrooms.[40] Their findings showed that students evidenced more indices of high-level comprehension (i.e., elaborated explanations) when discussing narrative texts. Further, in terms of text structure, students produced statistically significantly more authentic questions (i.e., another indicator of high-level comprehension) during discussions with texts written with a comparison structure than for other text structures (e.g., problem-and-solution). Based on this study, Li further investigated the extent to which text genre alone influenced the quality of discussions by conducting a study that controlled for text topic, prior knowledge, and perceived interestingness.[36] The results confirmed previous findings that students had more productive talk when discussing narrative text than expository text. A higher frequency of collaboration and co-construction of knowledge was observed among students during discussions with narrative text. In addition, she also discovered that individual students produced more elaborations when discussing a biographical or mixed genre text, compared to other text genres.

All in all, more research is needed to examine the role of text features in small-group text-based discussions. However, until such research is established, it is important for teachers to select texts for discussions—irrespective of genre, structure, or topic—that students have some background knowledge about as well as texts that allow for multiple interpretations so that students can engage in critical-analytic thinking.[19]

Guidance for Practitioners

- For text-based discussions, select texts that are level-appropriate, ignite interest, and allow for multiple interpretations so that students can engage in critical-analytic thinking.

CODA

Taken together, conducting high-quality discussions requires teachers to consider a wide array of contextual factors and to make pedagogical decisions accordingly. As examined throughout the chapter, factors such as group size and composition, learner characteristics, and text features exert considerable effects on the quality of classroom discussion and further impact the extent to which students achieve high-level comprehension and critical-analytic thinking. Moreover, in authentic classroom settings these factors often interplay with each other. For instance, students of similar ability levels may take different roles in heterogeneous and homogeneous groups, resulting in different learning outcomes. Thus, it is essential for teachers to acknowledge and embrace these individual differences to better facilitate productive discussions.

In the end, teachers make numerous instructional decisions in order to better prepare students to engage in effective, high-quality discussions. Many of these decisions can be likened to those that go into composing a jazz ensemble. As teachers consider the various contextual factors and call on the optimal elements of quality discussion they are in essence, coordinating individual students' unique instruments and rhythms to ensure a cohesive, compelling, and memorable melody.

REFERENCES

1. Vygotsky, L. S. (1978). *Mind in society: The development of higher mental processes.* Cambridge, MA: Harvard University Press.
2. Murphy, P. K., Wilkinson, I. A. G., Soter, A. O., Hennessey, M. N., & Alexander, J. F. (2009). Examining the effects of classroom discussion on students' high-level comprehension of text: A meta-analysis. *Journal of Educational Psychology,* 101, 740–764.
3. Murphy, P. K., Firetto, C. M., Wei, L., Li, M., & Croninger, R. M. V. (2016). What really works: Optimizing classroom discussions to promote comprehension and critical-analytic thinking. *Policy Insights from the Behavioral and Brain Sciences,* 1, 1–9.
4. Cao, Y., & Philp, J. (2006). Interactional context and willingness to communicate: A comparison of behavior in whole class, group and dyadic interaction. *System,* 34, 480–493.
5. Lou, Y., Abrami, P. C., & Spence, J. C. (2000). Effects of within-class grouping on student achievement: An exploratory model. *Journal of Educational Research,* 94(2), 101–112.

6. Webb, N. M., & Kenderski, C. M. (1984). Student interaction and learning in small group and whole class settings. In P. L. Peterson, L. C. Wilkinson, & M. Hallinan (Eds.), *The social context of instruction: Group organization and group processes* (pp. 153–170). New York, NY: Academic Press.

7. Kulik, J. A. (1992). *An analysis of research on ability grouping: Historical and contemporary perspectives.* Storrs, CT: University of Connecticut, National Research Center on the Gifted and Talented. Retrieved from ERIC database. (ED350777).

8. Lou, Y., Abrami, P. C., Spence, J. C., Poulson, C., Chambers, B., & d'Apollonia, S. (1996). Within-class grouping: A meta-analysis. *Review of Educational Research, 66*, 423–458.

9. Slavin, R. E. (1987). Ability grouping and student achievement in elementary schools: A best-evidence synthesis. *Review of Educational Research, 57*, 293–336.

10. Theberge, C. L. (1994, April). *Small group vs. whole-class discussion: Gaining the floor in science lessons.* Paper presented at the Annual Meeting of the American Educational Research Association, New Orleans, LA.

11. Wu, X., Anderson, R. C., Nguyen-Jahiel, K., & Miller, B. (2013). Enhancing motivation and engagement through collaborative discussion. *Journal of Educational Psychology, 105*, 622–632.

12. Liu, N. F., & Littlewood, W. (1997). Why do many students appear reluctant to participate in classroom learning discourse? *System, 25*(3), 371–384.

13. Mullen, B., & Copper, C. (1994). The relation between group cohesiveness and performance: Integration. *Psychological Bulletin, 115*(2), 210–227.

14. Festinger, L. (1950). Informal social communication. *Psychological Review, 57*, 217–282.

15. Murphy, P. K., Greene, J. A., Firetto, C. M., Li, M., Lobczowski, N. G., Duke, R. F., Wei, L., & Croninger, R. M. V. (under review). Exploring the influence of homogeneous versus heterogeneous grouping on students' text-based discussions and comprehension. *Contemporary Educational Psychology.*

16. Coldiron, J. R., Braddock, J. H., & McPartland, J. M. (1987, April). *A description of school structures and classroom practices in elementary, middle, and secondary schools.* Paper presented at the Annual Meeting of the American Educational Research Association, Washington, DC.

17. Torgesen, J., Myers, D., Schirm, A., Stuart, E., Vartivarian, S., Mansfield, W., . . . Haan, C. (2006). *National assessment of title I interim report to congress—volume II: Closing the reading gap: First year findings from a randomized trial of four reading interventions for striving readers.* Washington, DC: Institute of Education Science.

Retrieved from www.ed.gov/rschstat/eval/disadv/title1interimreport/index.html

18. Slavin, R. E. (1991). Synthesis of research on cooperative learning. *Educational Leadership, 48*, 71–82.

19. Wilkinson, I. A. G., Soter, A. O., & Murphy, P. K. (2010). Developing a model of Quality Talk about literary text. In M. G. McKeown & L. Kucan (Eds.), *Bringing reading research to life* (pp. 142–169). New York, NY: Guilford Press.

20. Azmitia, M. (1988). Peer interaction and problem solving: When are two heads better than one? *Child Development, 59*, 87–96.

21. Saleh, M., Lazonder, A. W., & De Jong, T. D. (2005). Effects of within-class ability grouping on social interaction, achievement, and motivation. *Instructional Science, 33*(2), 105–119.

22. Webb, N. M. (1980). A process-outcome analysis of learning in group and individual settings. *Educational Psychologist, 15*, 69–83.

23. Webb, N. M. (1991). Task-related verbal interaction and mathematics learning in small groups. *Journal for Research in Mathematics Education, 22*, 366–389.

24. Webb, N. M., Nemer, K. M., Chizhik, A. W., & Sugrue, B. (1998). Equity issues in collaborative group assessment: Group composition and performance. *American Educational Research Journal, 35*, 607–651.

25. Webb, N. M., & Palinscar, A. S. (1996). Group processes in the classroom. In D. C. Berliner & R. C. Calfee (Eds.), *Handbook of educational psychology* (pp. 841–873). New York, NY: MacMillan.

26. Tudge, J. (1989). When collaboration leads to regression: Some negative consequences of socio-cognitive conflict. *European Journal of Social Psychology, 19*(2), 123–138.

27. Johnson, D. W., Skon, L., & Johnson, R. (1980). Effects of cooperative, competitive, and individualistic conditions on children's problem-solving performance. *American Educational Research Journal, 17*, 83–93.

28. Saleh, M., Lazonder, A. W., & De Jong, T. D. (2007). Structuring collaboration in mixed-ability groups to promote verbal interaction, learning, and motivation of average-ability students. *Contemporary Educational Psychology, 32*(3), 314–331.

29. Fuchs, L. S., Fuchs, D., Hamlett, C. L., & Karns, K. (1998). High-achieving students' interactions and performance on complex mathematical tasks as a function of homogeneous and heterogeneous pairings. *American Educational Research Journal, 35*, 227–267.

30. Eder, D., & Felmlee, D. (1984). The development of attention norms in ability groups. In P. Peterson, L. Wilkinson, & N. Hallinan (Eds.), *The social context of instruction* (pp. 189–208). San Diego, CA: Academic Press.

31. Mugny, G., & Doise, W. (1978). Socio-cognitive conflict and structure of individual and collective performances. *European Journal of Social Psychology, 8*, 181–192.

32. Leaper, C., & Smith, T. E. (2004). A meta-analytic review of gender variations in children's talk: Talkativeness, affiliative speech, and assertive speech. *Developmental Psychology, 40*, 993–1027.

33. Webb, N. M. (1984). Microcomputer learning in small groups: Cognitive requirements and group processes. *Journal of Educational Psychology, 76*, 1076–1088.

34. Webb, N. M., & Kenderski, C. M. (1985). Gender differences in small group interaction and achievement in high-achieving and low-achieving classrooms. In L. C. Wilkinson & C. B. Marrett (Eds.), *Gender related differences in classroom interaction* (pp. 209–226). New York, NY: Academic Press.

35. Goatley, V. J., Brock, C. H., & Raphael, T. E. (1995). Diverse learners participating in regular education "Book Clubs." *Reading Research Quarterly, 30*, 352–380.

36. Li, M. (2017). *Examining the effects of text genre, prior knowledge, and perceived interestingness on students' acquisition of high-level comprehension* (Unpublished doctoral dissertation). The Pennsylvania State University, University Park, PA.

37. Alexander, P. A., & Jetton, T. L. (2000). Learning from text: A multidimensional and developmental perspective. In M. L. Kamil, P. B. Mosenthal, P. D. Pearson, & R. Barr (Eds.), *Handbook of reading research: Vol. III* (pp. 285–310). Mahwah, NJ: Lawrence Erlbaum Associates.

38. Meyer, B. J. F. (1975). *The organization of prose and its effects on memory*. Amsterdam: North-Holland.

39. Leal, D. J. (1992). The nature of talk about three types of text during peer group discussions. *Journal of Reading Behavior, 24*(3), 313–338.

40. Li, M., Murphy, P. K., & Firetto, C. M. (2014). Examining the effects of text genre and structure on 4th- and 5th-grade students' high-level comprehension as evidenced in small group discussions. *International Journal of Educational Psychology, 3*(3), 205–234.

Four

Learning Processes and Products

Propelling Students Ahead Through Talk

*Elizabeth M. Allen, Cristin Montalbano,
and Rebekah F. Duke*

The value of an education . . . is not the learning of many facts, but the training of the mind to think.

Albert Einstein[1]

Imagine two different students who receive an undergraduate degree in chemistry. Francisco has advanced through his schooling by accumulating a vast repertoire of factual knowledge, whereas Ruth proceeded through her education by honing a set of critical and analytic thinking skills. Francisco, who has memorized all 118 elements in the periodic table along with their atomic weight, family, and symbol, would be advantaged on factual knowledge tests and the Jeopardy game show. By comparison, Ruth, who has a greater capacity to think and reason about content, would clearly be advantaged when faced with the need to quickly find a solution to a unique problem. For example, consider how these students might react to a grease fire in their kitchen. Being armed with the capacity to think, Ruth would quickly move to smother the fire by eliminating the oxygen source with the lid from a pan. On the other hand, Francisco would likely spend valuable time trying to recall which substance is supposed to put out grease fires, for example, baking soda or baking powder. When called upon to think about, around, and with their knowledge of chemistry, Ruth clearly received the kind of education advocated by Albert Einstein.

As we have illustrated, the mere transmission of facts from teachers to students inadequately prepares them to meet the personal, professional, and societal demands awaiting them in the new millennium. Though it is imperative that students learn new information, they must also learn how to be strategic consumers of knowledge, equipped with the skills to critically analyze and challenge the information they encounter on a daily basis. As a result, educators are tasked not only with the responsibility of creating enriching opportunities for students to acquire a wealth of knowledge, but they must also equip students with the skills requisite for training the mind to think. Given these laudable responsibilities, scholars have begun to investigate various pedagogical practices in hopes of delineating those that are more likely to promote both critical-analytic thinking and enhanced learning outcomes. Among the instructional practices being explored is small-group classroom discussion.

Our purpose in this chapter is to explore study findings that illustrate the ways in which high-quality talk influences students' thinking, reasoning, and learning outcomes. Specifically, this chapter examines the impact of effective discussions on students' learning processes and products. To accomplish this purpose, we first overview the influence that talk can have on various cognitive processes, including critical-analytic thinking, argumentation and epistemic cognition, and relational reasoning. Then, we turn our attention to specific learning outcomes, including reading comprehension, content learning, and argumentative writing. Throughout the chapter, we forward guidance for practitioners gleaned from study findings.

TALK AND LEARNING PROCESSES

The term *cognitive processes* refers to purposefully applied thinking skills and strategies that foster deep learning and understanding of ideas and concepts. These processes enable students to critically analyze and question ideas and information, to interpret and consider various viewpoints, and to investigate patterns within various streams of information. Such processes can be explicitly taught and fostered through talk in classrooms. In fact, research has shown that high-quality talk is related to many cognitive processes, including critical-analytic thinking, argumentation, epistemic cognition, and relational reasoning.[2–7]

Cognitive processes can also be broken down into more specific sub-processes, including critical thinking. Critical-analytic thinking can be understood as the "effortful, cognitive processing through which an individual or group of individuals comes to an examined understanding" (p. 563) about a particular topic.[8] This examined understanding encompasses principles of argumentation,[8] such as the ability to present reasoning and evidence to support a position, as well as effective epistemic beliefs and practices, including thoughtfully analyzing the quality of content presented in various situations.[9–11] Relational reasoning, defined as "the ability to discern meaningful patterns" from seemingly unrelated information, is a precursor of critical-analytic thinking (p. 1).[12] High-quality talk about, around, and with text and content, facilitated in small-group discussions, is related to each of these cognitive processes and sub-processes. In the sections that follow, we review findings from the empirical literature on the influence of high-quality talk on students' cognitive processes, including critical-analytic thinking, argumentation and epistemic cognition, as well as relational reasoning.

Critical-Analytic Thinking

Due to the importance of fostering students' critical thinking and analytic skills, numerous investigations have explored the influence of various pedagogical practices on critical-analytic thinking.[4,13] Overall, the findings reveal that students' critical-analytic thinking skills can be improved through explicit and systematic pedagogical practices.[13–15] As a case in point, Quality Talk (QT) is an approach specifically geared toward fostering students' critical-analytic skills and high-level reading comprehension.[5,16] In a year-long study,[13] Quality Talk Language Arts (QT_{LA}) was delivered in two fourth-grade classrooms with thirty-five students in total. Analysis of video-recorded discussions reflected increased indicators of critical-analytic thinking (e.g., elaborated explanations and exploratory talk) over time—students' critical-analytic thinking skills improved over the course of QT_{LA} implementation. The results of this study suggest students' critical-analytic thinking skills can be enhanced through explicit and systematic pedagogical practices.

Argumentation and Epistemic Cognition

Argumentation can be understood as the presentation of reasons and evidence in support of a claim. The ability to engage in reasoned argumentation is a cornerstone of a democratic society,[17] as it fosters the ability to critically analyze ideas and information using sound reasons and evidence. Argumentation skills, however, do not develop naturally. Rather, such skills and abilities require immense cognitive effort and typically require explicit and systematic instruction.[18,19] As such, fostering students' abilities to engage in argumentation is imperative for ensuring students are prepared to meet the critical-thinking demands of society. Further, epistemic cognition, defined as students' beliefs about knowledge and knowing, is another cognitive process that fosters a deep understanding of ideas and concepts. Like argumentation, students' epistemic cognition can be enhanced through the implementation of effective talk in classrooms, and one way to stimulate students' epistemic cognition is through the use of argumentation.

Classroom-based studies have shown that high-quality talk can improve students' verbal argumentation skills.[2,20] In one particular study, two groups of teachers employed small-group, collaborative tasks in their classrooms, and the researchers instructed one group of teachers to use questioning to prompt students' argumentative thinking. In the groups where teachers used questioning, the student discourse contained more elaborations, reasons, and justifications for their responses, compared to the groups that did not receive questioning prompts.[2] Also, when teachers explicitly taught reasoning and argumentation skills to students, students had greater verbal argumentation skills.[20] Unfortunately, not all classroom discussions enhance students' verbal argumentation skills. Rather, verbal argumentation requires purposeful, instructional scaffolding combined with meaningful practice in small-group discussions.[2,20]

Argumentation skills can also influence students' beliefs about knowledge. For example, students who participated in an argumentation intervention had more refined beliefs about knowledge when compared to those who did not receive argumentation instruction.[21–23] Similarly, Ryu and Sandoval examined 8- to 10-year-old students receiving argumentation instruction and found statistically significant increases in their use of causal claims, evidence, and justification of thoughts by the end of the school year.[23] Therefore, it is important to understand that there is a relationship between argumentation instruction and students' beliefs about knowledge within a framework for high-quality talk. However, the research examining talk, argumentation, and epistemic cognition, as well as their interrelationships, is still emerging. What is overtly clear, though, is that it is vital to find ways to better prepare students to engage in these skills, as they influence how learners evaluate information and make decisions that not only influence their own lives but also the lives of others.[24] Accumulating evidence suggests that high-quality talk is a promising approach toward this end.

Relational Reasoning

Relational reasoning is another important cognitive process related to high-quality talk. Relational reasoning encompasses the ability to distinguish meaningful patterns within streams of information and is characterized by four different types of reasoning, including analogous, anomalous, antinomous, and antithetical reasoning (see Figure 4.1).[12,25] According to Alexander and colleagues, analogous reasoning is the ability to recognize similarities between dissimilar concepts. Anomalous reasoning, on the other hand, encompasses the ability to recognize a deviation from an expected pattern. Antinomous reasoning includes the ability to recognize instances of mutual exclusion between or among ideas, and antithetical reasoning incorporates the ability to recognize a relationship between two ideas, objects, or concepts that are on opposite sides of a continuum.[12,26–28] According to Alexander and colleagues, individuals who effectively use relational reasoning have a higher likelihood of achieving "depth and breadth of thinking" (p. 2).[12] Due to the importance of relational reasoning, it is essential to understand how various teaching practices may influence students' abilities to use relational reasoning.

Small-group discussion is one teaching practice with evidence for supporting students' use of relational reasoning. For example, students' use of relational reasoning in language arts and science classrooms during small-group, text-based discussions was related to productive talk.[3,7] In both of these

Text: *The Mystery of St. Matthew Island*			
Turn	**Speaker**	**Transcribed Talk**	**Codes**
1.	Samson	Ok. My question is what do you think would happen if we put predators on the island?	*Authentic Question*
2.	Alejandra	Well, I think that the reindeer would have more than they do right now, because they ran out of food because there were too many of them, and if they got rid of some of, some of them, then they would have a lot. They would have some food to spare during winter, maybe.	*Antithetical Reasoning*
3.	Roman	The predator would probably be eating the deer. And how I know that is because we read chapter five, and we've read and listened about the vines in deciduous forests. For example, the deer population was out of control, since their predators were being hunted by humans.	*Anomalous Reasoning*
4.	Norkeithus	Why do you think "The Mystery of St. Matthew Island" is like "Exploding Ants"?	*Authentic Question*
5.	Eva	I don't really agree, because "Exploding Ants" is mostly just - it explains all the different types of dangerous animals like exploding ants and stuff. But, in this story, it's when the reindeer start to go away, and it didn't really say too much information about them. What do you think, Daisy?	*Anomalous Reasoning*
6.	Daisy	Well, in "Exploding Ants" on page 91, it talks about predators. It talks about owls. And on page 354 and 355, they look like they talk about animals because there are two pictures of them, and then under there there's a little paragraph to read about it, I think.	*Analogous Reasoning*

Figure 4.1 Descriptions and examples of different types of relational reasoning[7]

studies, small-group discussions were conducted as part of the QT intervention. In the study on Quality Talk Language Arts (QT_{LA}), researchers selected and analyzed the discourse of three groups of fifth-grade students for instances of relational reasoning at three time points near the end of the QT_{LA} intervention. In the study on Quality Talk Science (QT_S), researchers selected and analyzed the discourse of two groups of high school physics students for instances of relational reasoning at the beginning and at the end of the intervention. Results of the study on QT_{LA} and relational reasoning indicated that analogous reasoning was the most frequently generated type of relational reasoning in the discourse and the frequency with which students generated instances of relational reasoning increased over time.[7]

In addition, high-level thinking questions prompted more instances of relational reasoning than other types of questions generated by students.[7] In the study on QT_S and relational reasoning in high school physics classrooms, researchers found analogous reasoning to be the most frequently generated type of relational reasoning. As was the case for students in QT-enhanced language arts classrooms, instances of relational reasoning increased in frequency from the beginning to the end of the QT_{LA} intervention. Further, questions that elicited affective response or a connection to prior experience elicited more instances of relational reasoning than other types of questions.[3] This is likely due to the fact that the question type prompts students to make links between objects or experiences.

In sum, numerous studies provide evidence that relational reasoning can be fostered through small-group discussions. Indeed, the aforementioned results indicate that students engaged in high-quality talk were more likely to discuss similarities between different concepts than to discuss concepts that deviated from an expected pattern, that were mutually exclusive, or that were on opposite sides of a continuum.[3,7] It is also important to note that specific types of questions were more likely to elicit relational reasoning than other types. Teachers may want to consider utilizing and harnessing these types of questions to elicit and enhance students' relational reasoning capabilities.

Guidance for Practitioners

- Provide students with explicit instruction on key aspects of critical analysis and argumentation prior to group-level practice through small-group discussion or individual-level writing.
- Promote students' relational reasoning by asking authentic questions and issuing challenges or prompts that encourage recognition of meaningful relations and patterns about, around, and with text and content.

PRODUCTIVE TALK AND LEARNING PRODUCTS

In recent decades, schools have come under increased pressure to provide substantial evidence of student learning. Although the focus seems to vary from year to year and relative to the particular curriculum standard, students' abilities to read and comprehend, acquire and use content knowledge, and produce sound verbal and written arguments have garnered a lion's share of attention in recent years.[29,30] No doubt, much of the concern is rooted in students' less than stellar performance on standardized assessments. As recently as 2011, the National Assessment of Educational Progress (NAEP) reported 70% of eighth-grade students did not achieve proficiency in science, and, in 2014, 85% of eighth-grade students did not show mastery of United States history content.[31] In 2015, 64% and 66% of our nation's fourth-grade and eighth-grade students, respectively, scored at or below the basic level in reading comprehension. In an effort to address this widespread underachievement, researchers have investigated pedagogical practices that can help improve students' reading comprehension, content knowledge, and argumentative writing skills.

As is the case with fundamental learning processes, classroom discussions and, more specifically, high-quality talk may also foster students' learning and product creation in different content areas. For example, the National Center for Educational

Statistics reported that eighth-grade students who had the opportunity to be involved in more frequent class discussions scored higher on their NAEP reading comprehension scores than those with less frequent opportunities for class discussions.[32] As such, researchers are beginning to focus on the positive impact that talk can have on reading comprehension, content learning, and argumentative writing. In the sections that follow, we explore the effects of small-group discussion on students' learning outcomes (i.e., reading comprehension,[5] content learning,[11,30] and argumentation writing skills[3]) in language arts, history, and science.

Reading Comprehension

The ability to read and comprehend is essential to understanding and building knowledge in an area of study like language arts or history. Importantly, the ability to read text or content is a necessary but not sufficient grounding for students to synthesize information or to make well-informed decisions. Students must be able to think about, around, and with the text and content that they have read. Throughout this book, we have referred to this type of comprehension as high-level comprehension. In the sections that follow, we overview the effects of high-quality discussions on students' basic and high-level comprehension in language arts and history.

Language Arts

Students' limited literacy skills have prompted scholars to examine ways that reading comprehension in language art classes can be improved.[5,13,33,34] For instance, Fall and colleagues studied tenth-grade students to determine how group collaboration influenced changes in students' understanding of text, with a specific focus on the facts of the story, the theme, and the feelings and motives of the characters.[33] There was a strong increase in students' understanding of the text from before the group discussion to after the group discussion. The authors concluded that group collaboration through text-based discussions increased basic reading comprehension.

During the last decade, researchers delineated different levels of reading comprehension (i.e., basic and high-level reading comprehension), and examined students' use of particular discourse structures and features and their influence on students' reading comprehension levels. For example, Soter and colleagues found that discourse features such as authentic questions, the number of reasoning words found in critical-analytic discourse, uptake, and elaborated explanations indicated high-level reading comprehension.[34] Also, students who participated in high-quality, text-based discussions that focused on the meaning and interpretation of text showed positive gains in reading comprehension.[35,36] Thus, when teachers implemented productive talk in the classroom, gains in students' reading comprehension were evidenced.[34–36]

Once scholars identified components associated with high-level comprehension from prior research, they began to develop approaches to help teachers incorporate these components in order to facilitate more effective discussions in their classrooms. For instance, Wilkinson and colleagues developed and investigated a successful classroom discussion approach called Quality Talk (QT).[5] An enhanced version of Quality Talk Language Arts (QT_{LA}) has been used in numerous classrooms with similar results.[13] Recently, the efficacy of three reading interventions were compared: QT_{LA}; Think before reading, think While reading, think After reading (TWA); and TWA/QT_{LA} Hybrid.[14] The results of this empirical study indicated that QT_{LA} and TWA/QT_{LA} Hybrid interventions effectively promoted high-level reading comprehension among fourth- and fifth-grade students. Given that TWA has previous, extensive empirical support as a successful reading comprehension strategy, the finding that QT_{LA} propelled students beyond TWA is striking.

History

Within the last decade, the extant literature has also begun to reflect investigations of reading comprehension within the context of text-based, small-group discussions in history classrooms. For example, Vaughn and colleagues designed and implemented the PACT intervention for eighth-grade social studies students in order to increase students' reading comprehension, among other goals.[37] The PACT intervention consisted of five interrelated components that included essential questions, key vocabulary, knowledge acquisition support, comprehension checks that were then used to facilitate discussions, and a knowledge application component. The knowledge application component was implemented near the end of the intervention, during which students engaged in text-based discourse to "clarify, apply, and extend understanding of text and content in a team setting" (p. 7).[37] The results of this study indicated that students who received the PACT intervention performed better on reading comprehension assessments than those who did not receive the intervention. Therefore, students immersed in scaffolded text-based, classroom discussion approaches in history classrooms outperformed peers receiving traditional teaching techniques on measures of reading comprehension. Together, these studies lend support to the importance of high-quality talk through small-group discussions in enhancing students' reading comprehension in both language arts and history.

Content Learning

Although much research involving small-group discussions has focused on literacy outcomes, other researchers have attended more closely to students' domain-specific or content-area knowledge acquisition.[11,30,38] What is clear is that students' mastery of historical and scientific content increases their ability to process and evaluate information from the news, media, and other sources, in order to make well-informed decisions. It also increases students' ability to address current environmental, health, and socio-scientific issues in their communities. Research pertaining to how small-group discourse has promoted content-specific knowledge acquisition and use is overviewed in the following sections.

History

Wissinger and La Paz explored whether small-group discussions promoted student content learning in history class.[38] Students were asked to read primary source documents and were then placed into small-group discussions. Half the groups were given critical questions and argumentative schemes to use during small-group discussions and the other half were not given any materials. After the discussions, students wrote arguments independently. Students who received the discussion materials learned more historical content when compared to the groups with no materials. Consequently, the use of scaffolded, small-group classroom discussions enhanced students' ability to process and evaluate information, such as primary source documents, in order to develop well-supported arguments. Engaging in small-group discussion, supported by the critical questions and argument schemes, allowed students to better develop their historical content knowledge and capability to process and evaluate information, which is necessary to make informed decisions in their daily lives.

Science

Chinn and colleagues were interested in the relationship between quality of argumentation structures used in discourse and students' science learning in a fifth-grade classroom.[11] They designed a study to examine whether the "quality of argument structure affect[ed] what students learn[ed] from discussions" (p. 81), specifically when looking at simple to complex argumentation structures, where a simple argument structure consisted of a claim and supporting reason. Further, they also developed a scoring rubric to measure the quality of students' argumentation structures during discussion; each student received an argumentation score according to the scoring rubric. The authors found a relationship between the quality of students' argumentation structures during discussion (i.e., argumentation scores) and their science learning scores. Chinn and colleagues concluded there was a positive relationship between students' argumentation scores and students' science learning scores. Students who used more complex argumentation structures during discussion had higher science learning scores. For example, a student who constructed a simple argument structure using only a claim and a supporting reason had a lower content learning score than a student who constructed a complex argument structure using a claim with supporting reason and evidence as well as a counterargument. Therefore, this study was an important stepping-stone because it demonstrated the importance discourse quality played on student learning, where the quality and complexity of argumentation structures used in discourse positively affects student learning.

Researchers have also explored the differences between group and individual argumentation. Specifically, how does the quality of group-level arguments compare to individual-level arguments and whether collaborative argumentation held in discussion formats influenced student learning when compared to individual argumentation? For example, Sampson and Clark designed an empirical study and assigned 168 high school students to either a collaborative or individual argumentation condition.[30] The authors examined three research questions to determine: (a) if groups produced better arguments than individuals, (b) how well the arguments produced in a group setting were adopted by individuals in the group, and (c) whether there were differences in the amount of individual content learning when working in a group versus alone. The students were presented an *ice-melting blocks* problem with six possible scenarios and were asked to determine the most valid explanation by choosing one of the six scenarios or generating one of their own explanations. Sampson and Clark did not find any differences between the two conditions in the quality of students' initial arguments. However, students collaborating and discussing in groups adopted and internalized some portion of the group's argument and demonstrated higher content mastery as well as a better ability to transfer their content knowledge and argumentation skills to novel problems, when compared to students working alone.

There are generally two main reasons why educators advocated for argumentative discourse within educational settings, particularly within a science domain.[17] The first reason is because individuals are expected to use argumentative discourse in critical life discussions and decisions—scientists also employ argumentation to arrive at models that represent real-life phenomena. The second reason is because argumentation has been shown to promote content learning. Indeed, in the preceding example, Chinn and colleagues found a relationship between argumentation and students' learning outcomes.[11] Likewise, Bathgate and colleagues examined how middle school students learned and implemented argumentation skills in scientific discourse. The results showed scientific discourse had a positive impact on learning outcomes in science and promoted argumentation skills.[39] Finally, other research has also shown that argumentation in discourse had a positive impact on student learning while investigating socio-scientific issues such as evolution.[40,41]

Together, the aforementioned studies provide accumulating evidence for our original premise that productive talk, facilitated in small-group discussions, promotes student learning. Specifically, when students are able to engage in argumentation as part of their discussions, they are able to engage in the high-quality talk that results in enhanced content learning in both history and science domains.

Argumentative Writing

Like reading comprehension or content learning, argumentative writing is also a key learning outcome for students to achieve during their educations. Argumentative writing requires individuals to weigh and communicate their logic and thoughts in written form, and undergirds civil and scientific literacy. Fortunately, like the other learning outcomes overviewed herein, argumentative writing can also be fostered through talk within a small-group setting.

Language Arts

Sweigart was one of the first to explore the effectiveness of different lesson formats on students' argumentative writing scores.[42] In his study, Sweigart investigated the impact of exploratory talk on twelfth-grade English students' argumentative writing, using different lesson formats: lecture, whole-class, or small-group discussions. The results indicated whole-class and small-group discussions resulted in higher argumentation writing scores than lecture, and small-group discussions were more effective than whole-class discussions.

In another study, Reznitskaya and colleagues were interested in understanding the impact of productive talk, through Collaborative Reasoning (CR) discussions, on students' argumentative writing in language arts class. Specifically, they examined six classrooms and assigned the classes to one of three conditions.[43]

Students in the first and second condition participated in four CR discussions. In the first condition, students only used CR, but in the second condition, the students used CR and were also given explicit verbal and written argumentation instruction halfway through. In the third condition, the class continued business-as-usual with no CR discussions. Student essays from all classrooms were compared, and students who engaged in CR had better argumentative writing scores than students who did not engage in CR. Furthermore, the CR-only group had better scores on argumentative writing than the CR group that received explicit argumentation instruction. However, students in the CR classroom with explicit argumentation instruction had better knowledge of argumentation principles than the CR-only and the business-as-usual group, where students in the CR-only group knew more than the business-as-usual group. Based on these findings, it was unclear whether the explicit argumentation instruction shifted the focus to argumentation principles rather than on constructing better argumentative writing. In addition, because students only participated in four CR discussions, it was unclear whether the length of the study may have influenced the findings.

Firetto and colleagues implemented a study specifically focusing on argumentative writing for students engaged in Quality Talk Language Arts (QT_{LA}).[44] Students in two classes received explicit instruction on the QT_{LA} discussion approach and on argumentation in discourse from the beginning of the year to mid-year and engaged in weekly discussions. After each discussion, students practiced argumentative writing. From the beginning of the implementation of QT_{LA} to mid-year, there was a statistically significant increase in students' argumentative writing scores, but the increases were not as high as expected. Consequently, in the spring, one class of students received additional scaffolded argumentative writing instruction while the other class continued to participate in QT_{LA} discussions without the additional instruction. At the end of the year, students in the class that received the additional argumentative writing instruction nearly doubled their scores from mid-year and had statistically significant higher argumentative writing compared to the group that implemented QT_{LA} without the additional instruction. The findings from this set of studies suggested that students from elementary school through high school have benefitted from engaging in high-quality discussions, specifically with respect to enhanced argumentative writing learning outcomes. However, the findings are somewhat mixed with respect to the need and impact of additional argumentative writing instruction.

Science

Within the domain of science, experts in educational research are currently exploring the relationship between productive talk and students' argumentative writing. Various studies have found that productive talk can increase students' ability to write relevant arguments, counterarguments, and rebuttals using text.[3,45] For instance, Grooms and colleagues conducted a small-scale study in two high school chemistry classrooms where one class used the Argument-Driven Inquiry (ADI) instructional model and the other did not.[45,46] Students who received the ADI intervention saw an increase their argumentative writing skills when compared to students in the non-ADI course.

Similarly, Greene and colleagues examined argumentative writing in high school physics and chemistry classrooms as part of their ongoing research on Quality Talk Science (QT_S).[3] Like teachers in QT_{LA}, they presented students with explicit instruction on the QT_S discussion approach and on argumentation in discourse. However, as part of QT_S, teachers also presented students with a series of model-based reasoning lessons about real-life essential questions, such as "Why do airbags have holes?" Within the small-group discussions that followed each model-based reasoning lesson, students were expected to consider the essential question by constructing and evaluating arguments through data exploration and previously read articles. The small group discussions afforded students a means to understand and challenge each other's arguments in order to develop the best normative explanation to the essential question. After the small-group discussions, students individually wrote out their arguments, and finally at the end of the lesson, the teacher shared the normative explanation through a whole-class discussion. Figure 4.2 shows examples of Rita's argumentative writing responses at the beginning of the year (Time 1) and again toward the end of the year (Time 5).

Across both language arts and science, small-group discussions with a critical-analytic framework have evidenced effectiveness in supporting students' argumentative writing. These findings have been manifest across a wide variety of students, regardless of age. Students from elementary school through high school have benefited from enhanced argumentative writing as a result of high-quality discussions.

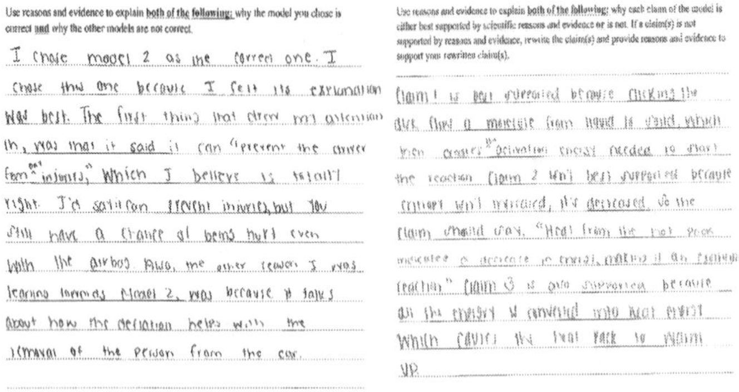

Figure 4.2 Rita's argumentative writing response at Time 1 (left) compared to Time 5 (right)

Guidance for Practitioners

- Employ high-quality, small-group discussions in language arts, social studies, and science, and encourage the use of group-level skills and abilities in individual work regardless of the content area.
- Set high expectations for students' oral and written comprehension, critical-analytic thinking, and argumentation in small-group discussions as well as individual assignments and products.

CODA

In this chapter, we first explored how productive talk influenced students' cognitive processes such as critical-analytic thinking, argumentation, and relational reasoning skills. The evidence emerging from relevant studies provided overwhelming evidence that small-group discussions can be employed as an instructional tool for promoting rich cognitive processing about text and content by students. We then reviewed learning outcomes resulting from participation in small-group discussions such as reading comprehension, content learning, and argumentative writing in language arts, history, and science. As was the case for cognitive processing, the studies revealed substantial improvement in students' oral and written products as a result of participating in effective, small-group discussions.

Further, it seemed that participation in small-group talk that encourages critical-analytic thinking and reasoning enables students to solve a variety of problems situated in varying contexts and content areas. Such findings provide substantive grounding for the chemistry scenario used to open this chapter. Indeed, whereas Francisco possesses stores of scientific knowledge, he lacks the critical-analytic and reasoning abilities of Ruth. Rooted in the studies overviewed in the chapter, we would definitely expect Ruth to be much more facile at responding to unique problems or relationally reasoning about complex, scientific challenges. Importantly, we would expect both Francisco and Ruth to enhance their understandings and performance as a result of participating in high-quality discussion about scientific challenges. In short, high-quality talk improves students' learning processes and products, and it is our sense that the ability to critically think and reason as a result of participation in small-group discussion represents the exact kind of pedagogical practice extoled by Albert Einstein.

REFERENCES

1. Frank, P., Rosen, G., & Kusaka, S. (2002). *Einstein: His life and times.* Cambridge, MA: Da Capo Press.
2. Gillies, R. M., & Khan, A. (2009). Promoting reasoned argumentation, problem-solving and learning during small-group work. *Cambridge Journal of Education, 39*(1), 7–27.
3. Greene, J. A., Murphy, P. K., Butler, A., Firetto, C. M., Allen, E., Wang, J., . . . Yu, S. B. (2016). *Promoting relational reasoning and scientific understanding through Quality Talk discourse.* Paper presented at the American Educational Research Association, Washington, DC.
4. Murphy, P. K., Wilkinson, I. A. G., Soter, A. O., Hennessey, M. N., & Alexander, J. F. (2009). Examining the effects of classroom discussion on students' comprehension of text: A meta-analysis. *Journal of Educational Psychology, 101*(3), 740–764.
5. Wilkinson, I. A. G., Soter, A. O., & Murphy, P. K. (2009). Developing a model of Quality Talk about literary text. In M. G. McKeown & L. Kucan (Eds.), *Bringing reading researchers to life: Essays in honor of Isabel L. Beck* (pp. 142–169). New York, NY: Guilford Press.
6. Murphy, P. K., Firetto, C. M., Wei, L., Li, M., & Croninger, R. M. V. (2016). What really works: Optimizing classroom discussions to promote comprehension and critical-analytic thinking. *Policy Insights from the Behavioral and Brain Sciences, 3*(1), 27–35.
7. Murphy, P. K., Greene, J. A., Firetto, C. M., Montalbano, C., Li, M., & Wei, L. (2016). *Promoting relational reasoning in elementary students' writing.* Paper presented at the American Educational Research Association, Washington, DC.

8. Murphy, P. K., Rowe, M. L., Ramani, G., & Silverman, R. (2014). Promoting critical-analytic thinking in children and adolescents at home and in school. *Educational Psychology Review*, 26(4), 561–578.

9. Greene, J. A., Sandoval, W. A., & Bråten, I. (2016). Introduction to epistemic cognition. In J. A. Greene, W. A. Sandoval, & I. Bråten (Eds.), *Handbook of epistemic cognition* (pp. 1–16). New York, NY: Routledge.

10. Murphy, P. K. (2007). The eye of the beholder: The interplay of social and cognitive components in change. *Educational Psychologist*, 42(1), 41–53.

11. Chinn, C. A., O'Donnell, A. M., & Jinks, T. S. (2000). The structure of discourse in collaborative learning. *Journal of Experimental Education*, 69(1), 77–97.

12. Alexander, P. A., Jablansky, S., Singer, L. M., & Dumas, D. (2016). Relational reasoning: What we know and why it matters. *Policy Insights from the Behavioral and Brain Sciences*, 3(1), 36–44.

13. Murphy, P. K., Greene, J. A., Firetto, C. M., Hendrick, B., Montalbano, C., Li, M., & Wei, L. (2016). *Enhancing students' comprehension and critical-analytic thinking through Quality Talk discussions*. Paper presented at the American Educational Research Association, Washington, DC.

14. Li, M., Murphy, P. K., Wang, J., Mason, L. H., Firetto, C. M., Wei, L., & Chung, K. S. (2016). Promoting reading comprehension and critical-analytic thinking: A comparison of three approaches with fourth and fifth graders. *Contemporary Educational Psychology*, 46, 101–115.

15. Abrami, P. C., Bernard, R. M., Borokhovski, E., Waddington, D. I., Wade, C. A., & Persson, T. (2015). Strategies for teaching students to think critically: A meta-analysis. *Review of Educational Research*, 85(2), 275–314.

16. Murphy, P. K., & Firetto, C. M. (2018). Quality Talk: A blueprint for productive talk. In P. K. Murphy (Ed.), *Classroom discussions in education* (pp. 101–134). New York, NY: Routledge.

17. Chinn, C., & Clark, D. B. (2013). Learning through collaborative argumentation. In C. E. Hmelo-Silver, C. A. Chinn, C. Chan, & A. M. O'Donnell (Eds.), *International handbook of collaborative learning* (pp. 314–332). New York, NY: Routledge.

18. Berland, L. K., & Reiser, B. J. (2009). Making sense of argumentation and explanation. *Science Education*, 93(1), 26–55.

19. Iordanou, K. (2010). Developing argument skills across scientific and social domains. *Journal of Cognition and Development*, 11(3), 293–327.

20. Zohar, A., & Nemet, F. (2002). Fostering students' knowledge and argumentation skills through dilemmas in human genetics. *Journal of Research in Science Teaching*, 39(1), 35–62.

21. Iordanou, K., & Constantinou, C. P. (2015). Supporting use of evidence in argumentation through practice in argumentation and reflection in the context of SOCRATES learning environment. *Science Education*, 99(2), 282–311.

22. Kuhn, D., Zillmer, N., Crowell, A., & Zavala, J. (2013). Developing norms of argumentation: Metacognitive, epistemological, and social dimensions of developing argumentive competence. *Cognition and Instruction*, 31(4), 456–496.

23. Ryu, S., & Sandoval, W. A. (2012). Improvements to elementary children's epistemic understanding from sustained argumentation. *Science Education*, 96(3), 488–526.

24. Hofer, B. K. (2001). Personal epistemology research: Implications for learning and teaching. *Educational Psychology Review*, 13(4), 353–383.

25. Alexander, P. A., Reading, T. D., & Laboratory, L. R. (2012). Reading into the future: Competence for the 21st century. *Educational Psychologist*, 47(4), 259–280.

26. Grossnickle, E. M., Dumas, D., Alexander, P. A., & Baggetta, P. (2016). Individual differences in the process of relational reasoning. *Learning and Instruction*, 42, 141–159.

27. Jablansky, S., Alexander, P. A., Dumas, D., & Compton, V. (2016). Developmental differences in relational reasoning among primary and secondary school students. *Journal of Educational Psychology*, 108(4), 592–608.

28. Dumas, D., Alexander, P. A., & Grossnickle, E. M. (2013). Relational reasoning and its manifestations in the educational context: A systematic review of the literature. *Educational Psychology Review*, 25(3), 391–427.

29. Forum, W. E. (2015). *New vision for education: Unlocking the potential of technology.* Retrieved from www.bcgperspectives.com/Images/New_Vision_for_Education_WEF_2015.pdf

30. Sampson, V., & Clark, D. (2009). The impact of collaboration on the outcomes of scientific argumentation. *Science Education*, 93(3), 448–484.

31. National Assessment of Educational Progress (NAEP). (2015). The Nation's report card. *2015: Mathematics & Reading Assessments.* Retrieved from www.nationsreportcard.gov/reading_math_2015/#?grade=8

32. National Center for Education Statistics (NCES). (2012). *The nation's report card: Findings in brief: Reading and mathematics 2011.* (NCES Report No. 2012–459). Retrieved from https://nces.ed.gov/nationsreportcard/pdf/main2011/2012459.pdf

33. Fall, R., Webb, N. M., & Chudowsky, N. (2000). Group discussion and large-scale language arts assessment: Effects on students' comprehension. *American Educational Research Journal*, 37(4), 911–941.

34. Soter, A. O., Wilkinson, I. A., Murphy, P. K., Rudge, L., Reninger, K., & Edwards, M. (2008). What the discourse tells us: Talk and indicators of high-level comprehension. *International Journal of Educational Research, 47*(6), 372–391.

35. Kamil, M. L., Borman, G. D., Dole, J., Kral, C. C., Salinger, T., & Torgesen, J. (2008). Improving adolescent literacy: Effective classroom and intervention practices. *IES Practice Guide*. (NCEE 2008–4027). Retrieved from http://ies.ed.gov/ncee/wwc

36. Shanahan, T., Callison, K., Carriere, C., Duke, N. K., Pearson, P. D., Schatschneider, C., & Torgesen, J. (2010). *Improving reading comprehension in kindergarten through 3rd grade: A practice guide*. (NCEE 2010–4038). Washington, DC. Retrieved from whatworks.ed.gov/publications/practiceguides

37. Vaughn, S., Swanson, E. A., Roberts, G., Wanzek, J., Stillman-Spisak, S. J., Solis, M., & Simmons, D. (2013). Improving reading comprehension and social studies knowledge in middle school. *Reading Research Quarterly, 48*(1), 77–93.

38. Wissinger, D. R., & De La Paz, S. (2016). Effects of critical discussions on middle school students' written historical arguments. *Journal of Educational Psychology, 108*(1), 43–59.

39. Bathgate, M., Crowell, A., Schunn, C., Cannady, M., & Dorph, R. (2015). The learning benefits of being willing and able to engage in scientific argumentation. *International Journal of Science Education, 37*(10), 1590–1612.

40. Asterhan, C. S., & Schwarz, B. B. (2007). The effects of monological and dialogical argumentation on concept learning in evolutionary theory. *Journal of Educational Psychology, 99*(3), 626–639.

41. Asterhan, C. S., & Schwarz, B. B. (2009). Argumentation and explanation in conceptual change: Indications from protocol analyses of peer-to-peer dialog. *Cognitive Science, 33*(3), 374–400.

42. Sweigart, W. (1991). Classroom talk, knowledge development, and writing. *Research in the Teaching of English, 25*(4), 469–496.

43. Reznitskaya, A., Anderson, R. C., & Kuo, L. J. (2007). Teaching and learning argumentation. *The Elementary School Journal, 107*(5), 449–472.

44. Firetto, C. M., Murphy, P. K., Greene, J. A., Li, M., Wei, L., Montalbano, C., . . . Croninger, R. M. V. (2016, April). *Using Quality Talk to foster transfer of students' critical-analytic discussions to their argumentative writing*. Paper presented at the American Educational Research Association, Washington, DC.

45. Grooms, J., Enderle, P., & Sampson, V. (2015). Coordinating scientific argumentation and the Next Generation Science Standards through argument driven inquiry. *Science Educator, 24*(1), 45–50.

46. Sampson, V., Grooms, J., & Walker, J. (2009). Argument-driven inquiry. *The Science Teacher*, 76(8), 42–47.

47. Chinn, C. A., Anderson, R. C., & Waggoner, M. A. (2001). Patterns of discourse in two kinds of literature discussion. *Reading Research Quarterly*, 36(4), 378–411.

Five

Quality Talk

A Blueprint for Productive Talk

P. Karen Murphy and Carla M. Firetto

In the previous chapters, we set forth the foundations necessary for engaging, high-quality discussions about text—discussions that lead to enhanced student learning. In this final chapter
we offer an overview of an approach to conducting productive discussions in the classroom that we have developed and
refined called Quality Talk. The primary goal of Quality Talk is
to enhance students' high-level comprehension about, around,
and with text and content; that is, the kinds of discussion that we
have referred to as effective or high-quality discussion throughout the volume. This means that students come to the discussion
with some knowledge *about* the text or content (e.g., main idea
and supporting details or basic understanding of a scientific phenomenon). Over the course of the discussion, students solidify
their understanding about the text or phenomenon, and through
the discussion they are encouraged to talk *around* and *with* the text
using probing questions and weighing claims, reasons, and evidence. Indeed, students are encouraged to share related personal
experiences, previously learned information, or shared experiences of the group. For example, a group of fifth-grade students
reading the story *At the Beach*, which is about siblings exploring an ocean reef on vacation, may begin by asking about the

main character's relationship with his siblings. As they progress through the discussion, one student may share a personal anecdote about her sibling and another student may reference a past science lesson about ocean reefs. The idea is that the kind of rich discourse that facilitates high-level comprehension and critical-analytic thinking occurs when students use the text or content as a jumping off point for productive talk in discussions.

This chapter begins with a brief history of Quality Talk and continues with a detailed description of the four core components of the approach. Whereas the findings from investigations of Quality Talk have been introduced in previous chapters, this chapter provides a comprehensive and thorough explanation of each of the main components and, where possible, figures showing classroom materials as well as excerpts from actual classroom discussions.

THE EVOLUTION OF QUALITY TALK

In 2002, Ian Wilkinson, P. Karen Murphy, and Ana Soter began examining classroom discussions. As part of this endeavor, they conducted an exhaustive review and synthesis of the literature on the existing researcher-developed approaches to small-group classroom discussions about text.[1] They were particularly interested in examining discussion approaches that had a peer-reviewed record of research. In their review, they identified nine approaches to classroom discussion meant to enhance students' comprehension (i.e., Collaborative Reasoning, Paideia Seminar, Philosophy for Children, Instructional Conversations, Junior Great Books Shared Inquiry, Questioning the Author, Book Club, Grand Conversations, and Literature Circles). After they identified the existing approaches, Murphy and colleagues analyzed the effects of the approach on the various forms of comprehension (e.g., basic or high-level). Having examined the effects of the approaches, Soter and colleagues solicited and secured discourse examples from proponents of each of the approaches and analyzed the nature of the talk.[2] When combined, the results of these two analyses allowed Wilkinson and colleagues to comprehensively examine key aspects of the various approaches.

We encourage readers to refer to the full publications of the aforementioned investigations; however, several notable findings served as an impetus for future research and are reviewed here. First, even though in the reviewed studies and discourse samples most of the approaches resulted in increased student talk (and decreased teacher talk), the increase in student talk did not necessarily result in concomitant increases in students' comprehension. Essentially, having students talk more during discussions was not enough to aid their learning—students needed to participate in what we have defined as productive talk. Second, although many of the approaches were successful at enhancing students' basic comprehension, few successfully promoted high-level comprehension. Indeed, although many, particularly efferent, approaches were successful at bolstering students' basic comprehension of the text, when focusing on critical-analytic thinking and reasoning, there was room for improvement. Finally, in terms of the discourse, there were numerous consistencies in the nature of talk for those approaches effective at promoting high-level comprehension. For example, those approaches showed higher incidences of authentic questioning, elaborated explanations, and exploratory talk. Hence, Quality Talk was developed by combining key aspects of the various approaches that appeared to enhance students' ability to think critically and analytically about, around, and with text and content. Details specific to the first iteration of Quality Talk are reported elsewhere—in general, the conceptual frame upon which the current iteration of Quality Talk is built remains largely the same as the initial conceptualization.[3]

In 2013, P. Karen Murphy was awarded two federally funded grants from the Institute of Education Sciences (IES) and the National Science Foundation (NSF). The IES grant focused on developing and refining the intervention in elementary school classrooms (i.e., fourth and fifth grade); we refer to this project as Quality Talk Language Arts (QT_{LA}). Specifically, the IES grant focused on developing a set of mini-lessons for teachers to use to teach their students the components of Quality Talk and to establish evidence about the ideal grouping composition for students taking part in QT_{LA}. The NSF grant focused on adapting Quality Talk for high school chemistry and physics classrooms; we refer to this project as Quality Talk Science (QT_S). The NSF grant focused on building upon the QT_{LA} project and assessing the efficacy of Quality Talk in a new domain and with a different population of learners. Where in QT_{LA} students may discuss narrative texts (e.g., *At the Beach*), QT_S students read about and discuss core ideas in science (e.g., energy, density, Newton's laws). For example, QT_S students may have a discussion as part of their chemistry class about the way in which a vehicle airbag deploys. The QT_S discussion may begin with a student asking *about* the type of chemical reactions that allow the airbag to safely deploy, information that is present within accompanying readings. As they progress through the discussion, students may begin to talk *around* and *with* the content: one student may share a personal anecdote about a time she experienced an airbag deploying and another student may reference a past physics lesson about momentum. Thus, QT_S is designed to enhance not only high-level comprehension of text but also scientific literacy and the building of content knowledge.

Overall, although the content and context vary, the core components of Quality Talk remain constant and are key to ensuring that students participate in discussions easily characterized as productive talk. Importantly, however, the research conducted as part of both IES and NSF grants has allowed us to refine the ways in which we understand, and teachers subsequently employ, the four components of Quality Talk in classroom practice. In the next sections the four components of Quality Talk, in its current form, are explicated with accompanying examples from the QT_{LA} and QT_S projects.

THE STRUCTURE AND SUBSTANCE OF QUALITY TALK

Before teachers can implement Quality Talk in their classrooms, it is critical that they understand the structure and substance of the four components that comprise the approach. To do this, teachers participate in an interactive, multi-day professional development workshop where they learn about each of the fundamental components of Quality Talk and how to enact these components in their classrooms. Details pertaining to the professional development and coaching are available near the end of this chapter, but as part of the workshop, we address the following four core components that depict the structure and substance of Quality Talk: (a) the ideal instructional frame for implementing Quality Talk, (b) the specific discourse elements identified as indicators of high-level comprehension, (c) the ways in which teachers can model and scaffold the discussions, as well as (d) the pedagogical principles teachers must embrace and employ as they implement Quality Talk. Each of these components is overviewed in the sections that follow in order to provide a comprehensive depiction of Quality Talk. Indeed, these components are built upon the theoretical framing forwarded in Chapter 1 and are securely grounded in the empirical literature established in Chapters 2 through 4.

The Ideal Instructional Frame

The instructional frame of any intervention approach outlines the structure for how it should be employed in practice. Thus, our *ideal* instructional frame outlines the ways in which we believe Quality Talk discussions are best employed. This frame is based on the existing empirical evidence, and it encompasses a variety of situations, settings, and specifications. Many of the central aspects of the ideal instructional frame result from the stance toward the discussion promoted in Quality Talk. Specifically, Quality Talk emphasizes a critical-analytic stance toward discourse. Yet, although a critical-analytic stance is core to Quality Talk, moderate degrees of efferent and expressive stances are still emphasized—students need to have knowledge about the text and content as well as an emotional or personal connection with it in order to achieve a critical-analytic stance. Whereas the resulting consequences of employing different stances are emphasized in much more detail in Chapter 1, details specific to the instructional frame of Quality Talk, as guided by the employed combination of stances, are herein described.

The teacher and students have specific roles within Quality Talk (see Chapter 2 for more on roles). Like much of the rest of the curriculum in a given classroom, the teacher chooses the texts and topics that will be discussed. As a case in point, in QT_{LA} the teacher selects and assigns the text (e.g., story or passage) that students will later talk about during their small-group discussions. The teacher may choose the text based on the extant curriculum (e.g., the main selection of the grade-level reading anthology), or she could select any other text that students have read (e.g., a supplementary book the students are reading) as the content for the discussion. Likewise, in QT_S the teacher also chooses the texts and topics, but generally, students read a set of short texts that are informational in nature and centered around a scientific phenomenon (e.g., nuclear fission). Quality Talk discussions can be based on texts of any genre, but there is evidence to suggest that mixed-genre texts may stimulate more productive talk (see Chapter 3 for more on genre).

After the teacher chooses the text, incorporating a pre-discussion activity will help to ensure that students come to the discussion with a grasp of the material and are prepared to talk. Based on numerous Quality Talk implementations, we encourage teachers to guide their students to think about the text genre, structure, and content, and to generate several authentic questions that they want to ask in the discussion prior to the discussion. Materials for both QT_{LA} and QT_S projects have been developed in order to ensure students have a basic comprehension of the content before the discussions and to support students' pre-discussion question generation. For example, in QT_{LA} a literacy journal guides students through several pre-discussion questions, including the process of identifying the main idea and supporting details of each text, and in QT_S students use a "catalyst" worksheet to examine different claims and the viability of evidence to support those claims. Both the literacy journal and the catalyst worksheet have space for students to write down their pre-discussion questions (see Figure 5.1).

As Quality Talk discussions take place in small groups of about four to six students, ideal composition of groups is such that they include students with varying ability levels (i.e., a mix of students with lower and higher abilities).[4] In addition, ideally the teacher is present in the group to facilitate the student talk. This is particularly important in the beginning as students gain familiarity with the approach. In QT_{LA} with students in primary school, the inclusion of the teacher in the discussions was particularly important, and we have encouraged our teachers to be present in every discussion with every group. To achieve this, teachers facilitated one small group of discussion, while the rest of the students completed an assignment or read silently. Then, when the first group completed their discussion, the teacher sat with the next small group, rotating through until all students participated in a discussion. With students in secondary school, there may

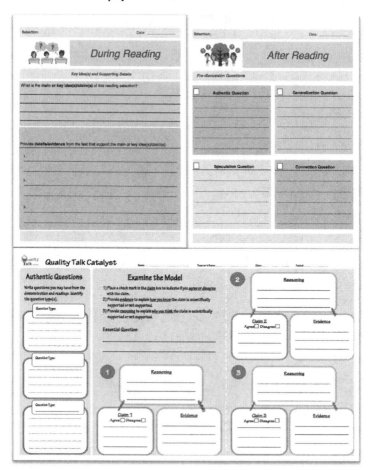

Figure 5.1 Excerpt of pages from the QT$_{LA}$ literacy journal (top) and the QT$_S$ catalyst worksheet (bottom)

be less of a necessity for teachers to facilitate every discussion. For example, QT$_S$ teachers facilitated one group, while another group independently had a discussion without the teacher. For our teachers implementing the discussions in this way, we provided two additional conditions. First, we advised teachers to remain with one group for the entirety of a discussion, avoiding "bouncing" from one discussion to another. In fact, such bouncing takes the teacher from being the metaphorical sun to a black hole where all forms of student engagement, interaction, and discourse are inexplicably drawn toward the teacher, unable to escape her gravitational pull. In a brief 15- to 20-minute discussion, it is particularly difficult for students to return to the "pre-event" level of discourse once the teacher has moved to another group. Second, we advised teachers to alternate which groups they facilitated, allowing the teachers to experience discussions from different groups and giving all students the opportunity to receive teachers' scaffolding. In such a scheme, it is particularly important that groups are formed heterogeneously with a keen eye toward emerging student discourse leaders. The literature is replete with examples of students taking on more of a teacher-facilitator role in the absence of the teacher. Leaders may emerge based on their intellectual prowess or their ability to socially negotiate the flow of the discourse among their peers.[5] In either case, it is important that the teacher not overshadow such leaders as they alternate between the groups from week to week.

It is over a series of Quality Talk discussions that a critical shift occurs from teacher to student—gradually, teachers release responsibility to their students. In fact, one of the key aspects of the instructional frame is that students in Quality Talk control the turn pattern of the discussion and take on the interpretation of the text; that is, the students take on interpretive authority. Instead of a teacher-directed turn pattern in the discussion, Quality Talk discussions are characterized by an open-participation pattern that allows students to call on each other, follow-up naturally about what other students say, and politely interject when necessary. Additionally, in Quality Talk it is not the teachers' responsibility to distill the essence or meaning of the text and content to the students. Students use the discussion to talk about the themes and ideas in the texts or establish the viability of the claims in QT_S about scientific phenomena. To do so, students are encouraged to draw on their varied prior knowledge or experiences and to challenge each other in the discussions in order to come to an examined understanding. See the excerpt of the teacher workbook in Figure 5.2 for an example of the difference between a teacher-directed pattern and an open-participation pattern of student discourse with students taking on the interpretive authority of the text.

Finally, after the discussion, incorporating both a discussion debrief and post-discussion activity can greatly enhance students' high-level comprehension and critical-analytic thinking. During the discussion debrief the teacher and students discuss how the process components of the discussion unfolded or not (e.g., asking authentic questions or everyone getting a chance to talk) and the extent to which the students adhered to the discussion rules (e.g., listening to what others have to say or showing respect). This brief conversation enables the participants to set goals for future discussions (e.g., a goal for some to participate more or less or a goal to stay more closely focused on the text as a source of evidence). In addition, this debriefing activity can be used to solidify students' understandings and ensure that any misconceptions have been addressed. Students' understandings are further solidified by the post-discussion activity. In QT_{LA}, the post-discussion activity involves students writing individual responses to an authentic question about the text requiring critical-analytic thinking and reasoning. This type of activity gives students an opportunity to transfer co-constructed ideas and interthinking from the discussion into a written response, thereby further honing students' ability to meaningfully think and reason. In QT_S, the post-discussion activity is designed to allow students to examine their understanding by reflecting on

Transcript #1 (Topic: Review of Newton's Laws)

Turn	Speaker	Notes	Word Count
1.	Teacher	All right, so, Newton's First Law of Motion - (14), summarize for us, very quickly.	14
2.	Student 14	Uh, an object (inaudible) acted on by a force, and an object at rest will stay at rest, (inaudible).	17
3.	Teacher	OK, and, um, what is inertia?	6
4.	Student 14	Um, resistance to change.	4
5.	Teacher	Good, All right, good job. Newton's Second Law of Motion. What does that tell us, (2)? Newton's Second Law?	19
6.	Student 2	It's the law of constant acceleration.	6
7.	Teacher	So (laughs) what does his Second Law tell us? Two parts to it. Somebody help (2) out. Newton's Second Law of Motion, the law of force and acceleration? OK, (4)?	29
8.	Student 4	Um, acceleration is directly proportional to force.	7
9.	Teacher	Good. That's the first part: acceleration and force are directly proportional. What's the second part? (3)?	16
10.	Student 3	An object will accelerate in the direction from which the force is applied.	13
11.	Teacher	That's right. Good. And so, Newton's Second Law of Motion, known as the Law of Force and Acceleration. (5), you want to summarize for it - uh, summarize for us again, just the, the two parts?	35
12.	Student 5	Um, well, force and acceleration are directly proportional.	8
13.	Teacher	Good, and ...?	2
14.	Student 5	(inaudible) the direction of the object (laughter) (inaudible) force - in the direction the force is applied.	13

Total Turns _____   Total Words _____
Teacher Turns _____ = _____%   Teacher Words _____ = _____%
Student Turns _____ = _____%   Student Words _____ = _____%
Total Questions _____
Teacher Questions _____ = _____%
Student Questions _____ = _____%
Describe the talk pattern(s) _____

Transcript #2 (Topic: What Determines the Color of an Object)

Turn	Speaker	Notes	Word Count
1.	Student 1	Why do we think that the wavelengths produce different colors?	10
2.	Student 7	I don't know. Does it have to do with something like energy? Or like maybe...?	15
3.	Student 1	(13), what do you think?	5
4.	Student 13	I think it has to do with the wavelengths.	9
5.	Student 1	Is it based on the light source? Because, like, when (8) moved that scale over, it ...	16
6.	Student 3	Well, different colors just have different wavelengths.	7
7.	Student 1	Yeah.	1
8.	Student 8	And then, the only thing that I have to say was probably very wrong, but it is just like different colors need certain, like, energy levels, or, like, certain things to be - just because, like, I think red - it showed, like, it was, like, 780 or something - nanometers or something. So depending on the type of wavelength - like, how many nanometers.	60
9.	Student 1	Yeah.	1
10.	Student 8	Depends on, like, the color that would be shown.	9
11.	Student 1	That sounds right.	3
12.	Student 22	Is it the higher frequency has the more energy? Is that right?	12
13.	Student 1	Yes.	1
14.	Student 22	So that would mean that purple would have the highest frequency, right?	12
15.	Student 1	Mm-hm.	1
16.	Student 22	Maybe that determines, like, the frequency	6
17.	Student 8	So we've come down to - it's maybe the energy and, like, the nanometers, and	14
18.	Student 1	Or the frequency	3
19.	Student 8	- also that it's - yeah, frequency. Other than that, I really am not very sure. Does anyone have anything else to say, whether you agree, disagree...?	25
20.	Student 1	I think that we got it.	6
21.	Student 8	We're good? OK.	3

Total Turns _____   Total Words _____
Teacher Turns _____ = _____%   Teacher Words _____ = _____%
Student Turns _____ = _____%   Student Words _____ = _____%
Total Questions _____
Teacher Questions _____ = _____%
Student Questions _____ = _____%
Describe the talk pattern(s) _____

Figure 5.2 Excerpt from a QTs professional development activity; two transcripts were included in the Teacher Coding Workbook as examples of different discourse patterns

the previously discussed claims and normative scientific reasoning and evidence relative to the key scientific understandings. In Figure 5.3, examples of the QT_{LA} and QT_S post-discussion activities are shown.

Figure 5.3 The top image shows an excerpt from the QT_{LA} literacy journal, which has two pages devoted to an argumentative writing activity for students to complete after reading and discussing the text. The bottom image shows the front and back sides of the QT_S Examining Your Understanding worksheet, devoted to supporting students' reflection on the essential question after reading and discussing the topic

Discourse Elements

One of the key distinguishing features of Quality Talk is its ardent focus on the nature of talk in small-group classroom discussions and the stringent belief that talk serves an external representation of cognitive processing. Rooted in the discourse analysis conducted by Soter et al., we know that certain indicators of high-level comprehension are evident in productive talk.[2] These elements can be roughly categorized based on whether they are in the form of questions or the responses to those questions. Quality Talk questions can be subdivided into major categories: authentic or test questions. As overviewed and defined in earlier chapters, authentic questions (AQs) are associated with high-level comprehension, whereas test questions (TQs) are more associated with basic comprehension or low-level declarative understandings. Further, these authentic questions can be categorized into three different types of authentic questions: (a) uptake questions (UTs), (b) high-level thinking questions (HLTs), and (c) connection questions (CQs). The discourse elements in the form of responses can be further refined into three types: elaborated explanations (EEs), exploratory talk (ET), and cumulative talk (CT). In the following paragraphs, each of these discourse indicators is described in detail with examples from Quality Talk discourse. Importantly, questions are categorized based on the nature of the responses they elicit.

Uptake questions are questions that build on a previous response or question. Unlike the other forms of authentic questions, these cannot be prepared in advance of the discussion, as they are inherently spontaneously generated based on the responses of others. For example, in the discourse excerpt in Figure 5.4, students in QT_{LA} were discussing a story about the RMS Titanic. The initial authentic question asked about how long one might stay awake at night in the water. Specifically, in turn 5, Renato built on a response by Johanna from turn 4 with

		Text: *The Unsinkable Wreck of the RMS Titanic*	
Turn	**Speaker**	**Transcribed Talk**	**Codes**
1.	Renato	How long are you going to stay awake?	AQ
2.	Johanna	Well you fall asleep when you get hypothermia.	
3.	Azhara	Which would probably happen pretty fast.	
4.	Johanna	No, it happens in like a half hour.	
5.	Renato	Well if that is true, then why didn't more people get hauled onto the lifeboats?	AQ/UT
6.	Merlin	Because they were probably full.	
7.	Renato	No, it says most of them were left only half full.	

Figure 5.4 Discourse excerpt from QT$_{LA}$ exemplifying an uptake question

an uptake question about why more people weren't saved by the lifeboats (see Figure 5.4).

High-level thinking questions stimulate generalization, analysis, or speculation in the discourse. These different elements of high-level thinking may occur independently of each other (e.g., students may engage in speculation without generalization) and still be classified as HLT. However, they may also co-occur, as evidenced in the discourse shown in Figure 5.5. The students were discussing a story about Leonardo da Vinci. In the passage, da Vinci began designing a full-size clay model of a horse that was destroyed during the French invasion, and the project was not finished in the artist's lifetime. In the discussion, Camille initiated the question event by asking other students to speculate what might have happened if the clay model was not destroyed during the invasion. As the students considered the various possibilities, each of them proceeded to reply in ways that indicated they were also analyzing the story (i.e., by picking out pieces of evidence from the text) as well as generating broad generalizations of da Vinci's well-being and happiness (see Figure 5.5).

Text: *Leonardo's Horse*

Turn	Speaker	Transcribed Talk	Codes
1.	Camille	What if the big horse did not get destroyed?	AQ/SQ
2.	Slater	Then I think, um maybe, like, he would have been a lot happier.	
3.	George	I don't think he would be as depressed and he wouldn't... Well, a little bit of the book would change, like, he would not have been dying for his horse and they wouldn't make another horse. They would not add that in the story. Like, I think they would have added a happier thing.	EE
4.	Camille	I think he wouldn't have been depressed because he would not have had to deal with one of his most prized possessions being destroyed.	
5.	Slater	Well, there is another part, he still may be depressed because he used all that metal and he would not have been able to finish it for a long long time. So when it was destroyed he did not have to look at it but having to see it unfinished may have made him even more depressed because he wants to finish it but he can't.	EE

Figure 5.5 Discourse excerpt from QT$_{LA}$ exemplifying the co-occurance of different elements of high-level thinking questions

Finally, connection questions stimulate the generation of connections to past experiences or texts. Importantly, the connections generated in response to these questions may be either individual (e.g., a family vacation) or shared (e.g., a class field trip). In the following discourse example (Figure 5.6), Brett asked a question that invited the rest of the group to talk about a school talent show that took place in one of the stories. As students answered the question, Yoko compared it to a talent show that had recently taken place in their school, and Nala also responded in a way that considered the differences between the two talent shows (see Figure 5.6).

Elaborated explanations are types of responses in which students provide multiple forms of support (e.g., at least two reasons

Text: La Bamba

Turn	Speaker	Transcribed Talk	Codes
1.	Brett	What did you think of the talent show [in the story]?	AQ/CQ
2.	Micaela	I think it went pretty well except for that part where the tooth almost fell off the stage.	
3.	All	Haha. Yeah!	
4.	Nala	It ended up good though, cause he made jokes and everyone laughed.	
5.	Yoko	I thought it was pretty funny when the toothbrush was chasing the tooth around the stage.	
6.	Nala	I thought it was a pretty weird skit but it would be funny to watch.	
7.	Earnest	I think it was a good talent show, but what they had to do in the talent show was like... childish, I guess.	
8.	All	Yeah.	
9.	Yoko	I think our talent show had a lot more singing and stuff like that in it. Or like, baton or whatever.	
10.	Nala	Yeah, like no one sang in that talent show.	
11.	Mrs. Pierre	At least in the part that we have heard of no one sang. We had a lot more singers, didn't we?	

Figure 5.6 Discourse excerpt from QT$_{LA}$ exemplifying a connection question

and/or evidence) for a claim. In Figure 5.5, when students discussed *Leonardo's Horse*, Slater responded to the authentic question on two occasions. The first time (turn 2), he responded with the belief that if the horse was not destroyed then Leonardo would be happier; initially, he provided no support for this claim. Later, after considering his peer's replies, he seemed to recall a different aspect of the story and changed his mind. In his second response (turn 5), Slater produced a different claim: that even if the horse didn't get destroyed Leonardo may still be depressed at the end of his life. To support this new claim, he provided multiple forms of reasoning and evidence to suggest that there may have been other factors involved in Leonardo's not being able to finish the horse and whether or not he would have been depressed. It is this later response that is classified as an elaborated explanation. In addition, it provides a convincing example for how elaborated explanations serve as indicators of high-level comprehension.

Exploratory talk is another indicator of high-level comprehension evidenced in productive discussions. However, unlike elaborated explanations where individual students produce the responses, exploratory talk is an *episode* of talk, which means it includes responses by multiple students across several turns. Episodes of exploratory talk are most easily characterized by an element of *challenge*; students challenge each other as they critically examine the ideas forwarded in the discussion. In Figure 5.7,

		Text: *The Unsinkable Wreck of the RMS Titanic*	
Turn	Speaker	Transcribed Talk	Codes
1.	Salma	And I was going to say, the person who built it, how do you think they felt when they heard that the Titanic sunk?	AQ/HLT
2.	Esteban	I think that they would feel very, very ,very, bad, like, I...	
3.	Casey	Especially when you are hearing that more than 1,000 people died because you built it wrong.	ET
4.	Esteban	Well, I don't think you can really go blame it on the person who built it. There's so many... a lot of... conducting things where people just kind of blame it on one person which they shouldn't because there are so many people in this, like, the person who was steering should have saw the iceberg and should have turned ahead or, like, should have seen it before then. The person who built it should have had to make it, like, better radar.	EE
5.	Casey	And, um, this huge, ginormous boat could not be built by just one person. Way more people should have worked on it, so, they can't just blame it on one person.	
6.	Esteban	They all could have built something wrong. And, um, the person who decided, "Oh, it is just so amazing! Let's just not, like, have enough life boats for everyone."	

Figure 5.7 Discourse excerpt from QT$_{LA}$ exemplifying exploratory talk

several students were discussing the aforementioned text about the RMS *Titanic*, considering how the builder might have felt after the ship sank. Initially, Salma and Esteban agreed that the builder would feel badly about the ship sinking because of all of the people who died. However, at turn 4, Esteban then challenged the idea of feeling badly and alternatively suggested that instead of the builder being at fault there were other people that should feel guilty about the role they played in the catastrophe. Casey continued to build on this idea by recognizing that a single person did not build the ship—the responsibility for the lost lives should be shared by many. What is evident within this episode is that students began to examine their understanding and think critically as they engaged in Quality Talk. Students were thinking about, around, and with the text.

The last discourse element is cumulative talk. Cumulative talk is similar to exploratory talk in that it is also evidenced across an episode of talk. However, unlike exploratory talk, cumulative talk involves multiple turns where students build on the ideas and contribute to examining an idea without the element of challenge. In Figure 5.8, the students were discussing what happens to neutrons that are released during nuclear fission. The students were considering the question while building on the responses of others, each adding a unique contribution, each adding a step on the group's assent toward high-level comprehension.

One of the unique aspects of our most recent iteration of Quality Talk relates to these discourse elements. In essence, we have come to understand that the teacher possessing knowledge of the discourse elements is not enough to enact productive talk during small-group discussions.[6] Indeed, students must also possess a thorough understanding of their role in the discussion,

Topic: *Nuclear Fission*			
Turn	Speaker	Transcribed Talk	Codes
1.	Mr. Báez	Is there anything else that [the neutrons] might do?	AQ/HLT/CQ
2.	Ju	Would they go to another atom, maybe? And then break that atom up and just keep going.	CT
3.	Kwame	Oh.	
4.	Ju	Like in a chain reaction.	
5.	Kwame	Oh yea, because if they went to go hit another atom, then it could create an even bigger explosion.	
6.	Ju	Exactly. So like, with the ping-pongs, you have one, and then when that splits you have three separate ones and then those go to other atoms and then those atoms split and it just keeps going and going.	
7.	Kwame	Oh. That makes sense.	
8.	Addy	So the [ping pong demonstration] would basically be the same as that [diagram in the article]? And then just keep adding three?	
9.	Ju	That's what I think.	
10.	Kwame	Yeah, cause it would just keep going and it would take three more. Oh, I just had like, a light bulb go off!	

Figure 5.8 Discourse excerpt from QT$_S$ exemplifying cumulative talk

including an understanding of the discourse elements. As such, in both QT$_{LA}$ and QT$_S$, teachers provided students with explicit instruction about each of these discourse elements through a series of mini-lessons. The mini-lessons and accompanying presentation slides, which were created by our team, included practice activities and animations with exemplars of the discourse. The teachers used the provided materials in order to ensure that the students were able to generate the specific types of questions that indicate high-level comprehension as part of the pre-discussion activity. See Figure 5.9 for a representation of the slides used by the teachers to teach questioning and argumentation in QT$_{LA}$ and QT$_S$.

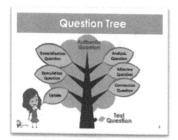 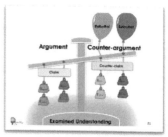

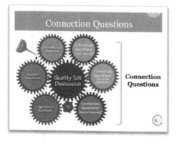 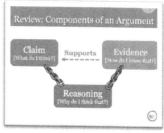

Figure 5.9 Four slides from the mini-lessons. The top row is from QT_{LA} and the bottom row is from QT_S. On the left side of each row is a slide depicting the types of questions taught in Quality Talk, and on the right side of each row is a slide depicting argumentation in the form of examined understanding (top right) and elaborated explanation (bottom right)

Teacher Modeling and Scaffolding

In Quality Talk, one of the fundamental functions of the teacher is to model and scaffold her students toward high-level comprehension and critical-analytic thinking. Though there are a dozen different teacher moves employed across the various discussion approaches (see Chapter 2 for more information), the specific teacher moves emphasized within Quality Talk are those that have been shown to enhance high-level comprehension and critical-analytic thinking. Five teacher moves are advocated in Quality Talk: summarizing, modeling, marking, prompting, and challenging.

During the professional development workshop, teachers are taught about each of these five teacher moves, as well as when and how to use them in their discussions. For example, teachers are taught to use more teacher moves in the first few discussions, to guide students into engaging in the kind of productive talk that is part of Quality Talk. As students become more familiar with Quality Talk, teachers are encouraged to use the moves more sparingly, as a temporary aid to the discussion. For example, a good time for teachers to engage in challenging is when a student states a misconception. Such a move urges the student to think a bit more deeply about the phenomenon and, hopefully, scaffolds remediation. In Table 5.1, examples from QT_S teachers

Table 5.1 Ideal Teacher Moves with Exemplars from QT_S Teachers

Teacher Move	Example from Quality Talk Science Teachers
Summarizing	Ok, so just to restate what you said, your issue is that you think there is reflection happening, and the model talks about refraction. So you think both are happening or just reflection or what?
Modeling	So if I was answering Emilo's question, just to show you how you do evidence and reasoning, I would say "Emilo, the reason that . . . the reason that you have to have the specific amounts of each element is because of the law of constant composition, as stated in the third article. It says that the law of constant composition states that the ratio of mass of the elements in a chemical compound is always the same regardless of the source of the compound. For example, water is always made up of 88.8% oxygen and 11.2% hydrogen . . .
Marking	[Directly to the student] Really nice explanation. You used evidence and excellent reasoning. You used two sources; you gave intertextual evidence, too, [turns to the rest of the students in the group] because he used the demonstration as well as using the article. Nice job on that.

(Continued)

Table 5.1 (Continued)

Teacher Move	Example from Quality Talk Science Teachers
Prompting	So, is there any evidence you can add from either the readings or the videos that mass does not affect their fall?
Challenging	You have light penetrating through [the screen], so why isn't the whole screen lighting up. What's with the dark spots? . . . [student replies] If that's the case, then why are there seven or eight bright spots on the screen.

are provided for each of the five teacher moves. In all cases, what is important is that the moves reinforce students' productive talk toward high-level comprehension and deep, meaningful content learning about, around, and with text or content.

Pedagogical Principles

A set of five pedagogical principles makes up the fourth and final component of the Quality Talk model. Individually, each principle encompasses a core idea about teaching and learning requisite for stimulating productive talk about text and content. When internalized by teachers, this set of beliefs can facilitate a dialogically rich, safe space for discussion in the classroom.

Of the five principles, the first and foremost is that *language is a tool for thinking and interthinking*. As mentioned in Chapter 1, the idea behind this principle is that teachers understand and value the talk that students are engaging in as part of the Quality Talk discussions. It is critical that teachers embrace the actual process of talking as a way of thinking, both individually and as a group, as it can then be internalized by those engaged in the discussion. This principle is deeply rooted in work by Vygotsky and is situated within the sociocognitive and sociocultural theoretical frameworks.[7]

Rules	How do we participate in Quality Talk?
- We don't need to raise hands. - We talk one at a time. - We give others time to speak. - We listen to each other. - We respect others' opinions. - We consider or think about others' ideas. - We give reasons to explain our ideas. - We question/argue about ideas not people. - If we disagree, we ask "Why?"	· We don't need to raise our hands. · We talk one at a time. · We share our ideas and listen to each other. · We give reasons to explain ideas. · We respect others' opinions. · We question or argue about ideas not people. · We consider others' ideas. · If we disagree, we ask *"Why do you think so?"* or *"How do you know that?"*

Figure 5.10 Rules for Quality Talk are presented in the slides during the first lesson in both the QT$_{LA}$ (left) and QT$_S$ (right)

The second pedagogical principle relates to *normative discourse expectations and dialogic responsiveness*. Specifically, the normative discourse expectations are manifest for the students in the form of ground rules (see Figure 5.10). These rules are designed to support and promote productive talk in the discussions by encouraging the open-participation pattern characteristic of Quality Talk (e.g., *"We don't need to raise hands."* or *"We talk one at a time."*). In addition, ground rules also promote the types of responses that move students toward high-level comprehension and critical-analytic thinking. For example, to promote elaborated explanations, one of the rules states: *"We give reasons to explain our ideas,"* and to promote exploratory talk one of the rules states, *"If we disagree, we ask, 'Why do you think that?' or 'How do you know that?'"* Importantly, in order for students to understand and adopt these rules, teachers are encouraged to briefly review the rules before each discussion and to debrief on their use following the discussions.

As students become more familiar with the normative discourse expectations set forth in the ground rules, the teachers are able to engage in dialogic responsiveness by gradually releasing responsibility of the discussion and interpretive authority to the students. Initially, students may be unfamiliar with the act of open-participation models in the classroom—they may raise their hands automatically to answer a question, even though they know that they do not need to do so. Thus, in the beginning, teachers may have a more active role in order to engage students in productive talk. They may model authentic questioning for the students or prompt students to elaborate on their responses. However, as students become more familiar with Quality Talk, teachers begin to talk less and less, encouraging students to talk amongst themselves and gradually releasing responsibility to the students. During this time, the students may still consider the teacher the authority and care should be taken for the teacher to listen rather than to contribute in the discussions. After students become well versed in engaging in Quality Talk discourse, the teacher may then re-enter the discussion as a participant, rather than as the authority. This may allow her to use carefully selected teacher moves that further enhance students' high-level comprehension and critical-analytic thinking, while maintaining a primarily observational role in the discussions.

Building off of the previous principle, the third principle is that as teachers facilitate discussions they must *balance responsiveness and structure*. This means that students' talk necessarily deviates from being exclusively *about* the text, as they candidly share connections or personal anecdotes *around* and *with* the text. However, it is not always overtly clear when the discourse has veered too far astray from the text or topic. It may be difficult to identify the exact point in which a discussion moves too far afield (e.g., planning social activities after school), in order for it to be reframed and refocused effectively. Indeed, facilitating small-group discussions requires teachers to be ever cognizant of the balancing act between allowing students the freedom to make contributions that add to the discussion with the structure and focus necessary to ensure productive learning about the text or topic.

The fourth principle involves ensuring teachers have content clarity. In essence, it is important that teachers have strong knowledge of the text and content prior to the discussion, and they must also possess a well-formed idea of the key content students need to acquire during the discussion. For example, one of the QT_S content lessons focuses on intermolecular forces, where the essential question of the lesson is: *Why does Vaseline dissolve in soapy water but not pure water?* Indeed, even though students may spend time in the discussion talking and learning about, around, and with various concepts covered in texts they read before the discussion (e.g., solvents, polar and nonpolar molecules, or hydrogen bonding), all students should leave the discussion able to meaningfully respond to the essential question with reasons and evidence. When discussion groups include students of all ability levels (i.e., heterogeneous ability-level grouping, see Chapter 3), they should be able to navigate toward answering the essential questions, even without support from the teacher, once they become familiar with Quality Talk. However, teachers should be prepared to provide additional guidance and support, if necessary. One way teachers may be able to do this is by preparing a set of "back-pocket questions" in advance of the discussion. These questions may be particularly useful in instances where students veer off topic. Instead of saying, "please get back on topic," a teacher could quickly redirect the conversation by asking a pre-prepared question. In sum, just as students benefit when they come to the discussions having completed pre-discussion activities, students also benefit when their teachers come to the discussions prepared with content clarity.

The fifth and final pedagogical principle is that teachers need to *embrace space* and diversity within the discourse. Each and every student in the classroom brings a unique, individual perspective to the discussion—students each bring their own combination of prior knowledge and experiences. For example, in QT_{LA} when a teacher facilitates three different discussions on the story *Leonardo's Horse*, the goal should not be to have three identical conversations all arriving to the same consensus of whether Leonardo da Vinci was fulfilled at the end of his life. One student may share her experience seeing the *Mona Lisa* while visiting the Louvre Museum, whereas another may share a description of information from a documentary he watched about da Vinci. Students' individual experiences should be recognized and celebrated. This diversity extends to individuals' culture and language, as well as to the context of the school and community (e.g., urban or rural, low or high socioeconomic status). For example, discussions conducted about the text *At the Beach* would naturally be different for a group of students enrolled in an urban, public school on the California coast compared to a group of students from a rural, private school in Kansas. Indeed, the weaving of individual students' perspectives and backgrounds means that no two discussions will ever be exactly the same, not unlike a hand-woven piece of fabric.

As we continue expanding Quality Talk, it is this final principle that becomes the core of our research. We are collaborating with international colleagues to recontextualize Quality Talk for implementation in other countries, including South Africa and Taiwan. We recognize that we must acknowledge, and embrace, the unique contexts afforded by each, in order to result in richer, more meaningful discussions.

SUCCESSFULLY ENACTING QUALITY TALK

As mentioned earlier, teachers learn about the four components of Quality Talk while participating in a professional development workshop, before they begin implementing it in their classrooms. However, enacting Quality Talk with fidelity (i.e., in a way consistent with prior research that has been proven effective) requires both initial and *ongoing* professional development. In earlier research, Wilkinson and colleagues studied fourteen language arts teachers as they implemented Quality Talk over the course of the school year.[8] Although all of the teachers participated in the initial professional development sessions at the beginning of the school year, only half were provided with additional, ongoing training throughout the year. These seven teachers received an additional three follow-up sessions as well as in-class coaching. At the end of the year, students from the classes of teachers who had the extra professional development scored higher on a test of persuasive writing than students from classes where the teachers only had the initial professional development. Essentially, this suggests that initial and ongoing professional development for teachers may result in implementation of discussion that produces better learning outcomes for students.

As part of both QT_{LA} and QT_S projects, the content and delivery of the Quality Talk professional development has been iteratively refined over the past several years. Specifically, each year we have taken advantage of the rich, constructive feedback provided by participating teachers as well as our empirical data to enhance the professional development experience in subsequent years. As a result, the final iteration of the professional development, described in the following sections, was strongly endorsed by teachers, and fidelity data also indicated that teachers successfully implemented Quality Talk—implementation that continued beyond the life of the funded projects.

In the initial, two-day professional development workshop, teachers learn about each of the four components of Quality Talk as well as how to enact these components in their classrooms. Throughout the workshop, videos of Quality Talk in action and transcripts of the discourse, like those presented earlier in the chapter, serve as concrete examples. As a case in point, following the presentation of the two types of discourse patterns (i.e., teacher-directed and open-participation), two exemplar transcripts are provided to the teachers (see Figure 5.2). After reading the two transcripts, as a group we discuss some of the similarities and differences between the discussions, while concluding with the idea that Quality Talk utilizes the open-participation pattern.

One of the unique aspects of Quality Talk that results from the initial and ongoing professional development is that not only do teachers learn *about* the discourse elements, but they actually begin to identify these indicators of high-level comprehension in the discourse in real time. Basically, Quality Talk teachers learn how to *code* talk as it unfolds in the discussion. We support this by utilizing extensive practice in the initial professional development workshop. First, teachers practice identifying only authentic and test questions in discourse transcripts. Later, they examine the transcripts to see if any of the authentic questions have secondary codes (e.g., connection questions), and finally, they return to these transcripts to see if the responses also contain evidence of elaborated explanations, exploratory talk, or cumulative talk. During the sessions, the teachers first read discourse transcripts, then they hear the audio recordings of the transcripts, and then they watch the discourse unfold through the use of video recordings. The idea is that we scaffold teachers' ability to discern what the talk means for when they are facilitating discussions in their own classrooms.

After the initial professional development workshop, teachers meet with discourse coaches approximately once a month as they implement Quality Talk. Prior to the coaching session, teachers prepare by engaging in independent reflection and coding of discourse from their own classrooms. This allows teachers an opportunity to carefully reflect upon whether their students are displaying these indicators of high-level comprehension. During the coaching sessions, teachers collaboratively review their coded discourse excerpts (i.e., from one of their own recent discussions) with Quality Talk coaches in a positive and encouraging environment. Teachers and discourse coaches talk about teachers' successes, troubleshoot their challenges, and set goals for future discussions.

As teachers become increasingly facile with coding, they are able to identify the key discourse indicators in the talk as it is unfolding during the Quality Talk discussions. This allows teachers to actively regulate their facilitation of the discussion. They can identify when the discourse is excelling, allowing them to sit back and watch students think critically and analytically, and they can recognize when the discourse is faltering, at which time they may choose to use a teacher move or back-pocket question to reframe the talk.

FIDELITY AND FEEDBACK OF QUALITY TALK

The success of any intervention approach requires that it be implemented effectively in the classroom. To do so, teachers must strike a balance between enacting Quality Talk in their classrooms in a way that is consistent with the aforementioned components and enacting Quality Talk in their classrooms in a way that is authentic to their environment (i.e., embracing their own space).[9] Although major deviations from the protocol (e.g., trying to engage in whole class Quality Talk discussions) may not result in the types of learning gains we have seen in our research, smaller personalizations (e.g., selecting a culturally appropriate text to discuss) sensitive to the constraints of one's particular context is encouraged to enhance implementation.[10] Participation in the Quality Talk professional development and coaching helps to support high-fidelity implementation of Quality Talk. Indeed, as part of the research we have conducted thus far, all of our teachers had extensive knowledge of the model and more knowledge than comparison teachers. Inspection of the video-recorded observations showed high adherence to the model.[11,12]

Formal feedback from participating teachers suggested that they perceived the lessons and discussions to be an effective use of instructional time and that Quality Talk resulted in increases in their students' comprehension of texts and content. Formal feedback from students regarding their perceptions of Quality Talk was also gathered. Across three cohorts of students participating in Quality Talk, students consistently reported that they enjoyed engaging in the discussions and said that they learned a lot from the discussions.[11]

CODA

In the end, Quality Talk is designed to give rise to productive talk about, around, and with text and content in which control of the discussion and interpretive authority is gradually released to students. Thus far, we have only shared our views and research pertaining to the Quality Talk approach. No doubt, we are particularly biased in this regard.

As researchers, we often have the opportunity to listen to students engaging in Quality Talk discussions. Hearing these students engaging in such complex, cognitive processes and *training the mind to think*[13] is both inspiring and rewarding. For us, listening to an effective Quality Talk discussion is similar to an avid sports fan watching the Chicago Cubs win the World Series or a music aficionado experiencing the timeless melodies of a jazz quartet in the French Quarter. Indeed, like sports fans and music aficionados, we are drawn to watching teachers and students seamlessly transitioning roles over the duration of the school year, like players on a team, and hearing students contributing high-level verbalizations and building on others' responses, like jazz musicians. As such, we chose to close this chapter, and subsequently this book, by giving voice to individuals who were instrumental in the development and refinement of the approach. Specifically, the concluding quotes offer an apt appraisal of the utility of Quality Talk from the perspective of a language arts student as well as a teacher's thoughts regarding the value and impact of Quality Talk Science on her students.

> Even if you don't realize it, [Quality Talk] is actually a mixture of three different subjects: writing, English, and reading. Cause, like, it teaches you the right words to use, so that would be the English, and it helps you to write, so that would be the writing, and it helps you to comprehend.
>
> —Fifth-Grade QT_{LA} Student

> My students have changed a lot, they're a lot more willing to give their ideas and feel more confident because they know how to find evidence and reasoning to support their ideas. I have one particular student who was very outspoken and very authoritative, and the kids were afraid at the beginning of the year to challenge anything that he said. They felt that he was the authority and that whatever he said was definitely correct. I find it interesting now how they challenge him. And he can no longer just make a statement, but he actually has to have some evidence to support what he is saying.
>
> —QT_S Chemistry Teacher

REFERENCES

1. Murphy, P. K., Wilkinson, I. A. G., Soter, A. O., Hennessey, M. N., & Alexander, J. F. (2009). Examining the effects of classroom discussion on students' high-level comprehension of text: A meta-analysis. *Journal of Educational Psychology, 101*, 740–764. http://dx.doi.org/10.1037/a0015576

2. Soter, A. O., Wilkinson, I. A. G., Murphy, P. K., Rudge, L., Reninger, K., & Edwards, M. (2008). What the discourse tells us: Talk and indicators

of high-level comprehension. *International Journal of Educational Research, 47*, 372–391. http://dx.doi.org/10.1016/j.ijer.2009.01.001

3. Wilkinson, I. A. G., Soter, A. O., & Murphy, P. K. (2010). Developing a model of Quality Talk about literary text. In M. G. McKeown & L. Kucan (Eds.), *Bringing reading research to life* (pp. 142–169). New York, NY: Guilford Press.

4. Murphy, P. K., Greene, J. A., & Firetto, C. M. (2016, December). *A quantitative and qualitative examination of homogeneous and heterogeneous grouping in classroom discourse*. Poster presented at the Institute of Education Sciences Annual Principal Investigators Meeting, Washington, DC.

5. Anderson, R. C., Nguyen-Jahiel, K., McNurlen, B., Archodidou, A., Kim, S., Reznitskaya, A., & Gilbert, L. (2001). The Snowball Phenomenon: Spread of ways of talking and ways of thinking across groups of children. *Cognition and Instruction, 19*(1), 1–46. http://dx.doi.org/10.1207/S1532690XCI1901_1

6. Reninger, K. B., & Wilkinson, I. A. G. (2010). Using discussion to promote striving readers' higher level comprehension of literary texts. In J. L. Collins & T. G. Gunning (Eds.), *Building struggling students' higher level literacy: Practical ideas, powerful solutions* (pp. 57–83). Newark, DE: International Reading Association.

7. Vygotsky, L. (1978). *Mind in society: The development of higher psychological processes*. Cambridge, MA: Harvard University Press.

8. Wilkinson, I. A. G., Soter, A. O., Murphy, P. K., & Li, J. (2008, March). *Promoting high-level comprehension of text through quality talk: A quasi-experimental study*. Paper presented at the Annual Meeting of the American Educational Research Association, New York, NY.

9. Murphy, P. K. (2015). Mooring points and touchstones along the road to school-based interventions—An introduction. *Contemporary Educational Psychology, 40*, 1–4. doi:10.1016/j.cedpsych.2014.10.003

10. Murphy, P. K., Firetto, C. M., Li, M., Wei, L., & Croninger, R. C. V. (2017). Fostering student writing through intervention research: An examination of key components. In R. Fidalgo & T. Olive (Series Eds.) & R. Fidalgo, K. R. Harris, & M. Braaksma, (Vol. Eds.), *Studies in Writing Series: Vol. 34., Design principles for teaching effective writing*, (pp. 253-279). Leiden, NL: Brill. doi:10.1163/9789004270480_012

11. Murphy, P. K., Greene, J. A., & Firetto, C. M. (2015). *Quality Talk: Developing students' discourse to promote critical-analytic thinking, epistemic cognition, and high-level comprehension*. (Technical Report No. 2). University Park, PA: The Pennsylvania State University.

12. Murphy, P. K., Greene, J. A., Butler, A., & Criswell, B. A. (2015). *Integrating Quality Talk professional development to enhance professional vision and leadership for STEM teachers in high-need schools.* (Technical Report No. 2). University Park, PA: The Pennsylvania State University.

13. Frank, P., Rosen, G., & Kusaka, S. (2002). *Einstein: His life and times.* Cambridge, MA: Da Capo Press.

Argumentation	the process of presenting reasons and evidence to support a claim, usually manifested in oral/verbal or written form; see also *Written argumentation* and *Verbal argumentation* (Ch. 1, 4)
Argumentative writing	see *Written argumentation* (Ch. 4)
Authentic question	a question for which no exact answer is known; can usually be answered in different ways (Ch. 2, 3, 4)
Biographical text	a text that describes a person's life and experiences (Ch. 3)
Cognitive process	the process of thinking (Ch. 4)
Cognitive skills	skills used by your brain to perform mental activities, such as learning, reading, thinking, etc. (Ch. 4)
Cognitive theory	defines learning as the assimilation, integration, or incorporation of new information that results in the reorganization of cognitive structures (Ch. 1)
Comprehension	the automatic construction of meaning (Ch. 1)
Connection question	a question that elicits a reference to other literary or nonliterary works, data, works of art, other multimedia, the Internet, television, newspapers, or magazines (Ch. 2, 3, 5)
Content	the knowledge contained within a specific area, such as science, language arts, or history (Ch. 4)

Critical-analytic stance a stance that encourages students to consider what the underlying assumptions of a text are by thinking about, around, and with the text (Ch. 1)

Critical-analytic thinking effortful, cognitive processing through which an individual or group of individuals comes to an examined understanding about a particular topic (Ch. 3, 4)

Deductive reasoning to break down concepts, ideas, or arguments rather than to build up ideas (Ch. 2)

Discourse a form of spoken communication, discussion, or debate (Ch. 4)

Discussion engagement the level of participation and interest a student has in a discussion (Ch. 3)

Domain an area of knowledge (Ch. 4)

Efferent stance a stance that encourages students to focus on gaining and retrieving as much information from a text as possible (Ch. 1)

Elaborated explanation answers that are built upon extended statements with reasons and evidence (Ch. 2, 3)

Epistemic belief belief about knowledge and knowing (Ch. 2)

Epistemic cognition encompasses the thought processes people use as they acquire, understand, justify, change, and use knowledge in formal and informal contexts (Ch. 4)

Evidence information from experience, texts, and other sources that supports a student's reasons (Ch. 1)

Exploratory talk students co-construct and share knowledge over several turns, evaluate evidence, and consider alternatives (Ch. 2)

Expository text a text written for the purpose of conveying information and facts (Ch. 3)

Expressive stance a stance that encourages students to consider their experiences or emotional response to a text (Ch. 1)

Fidelity	the degree to which an implementation of a program or intervention is consistent with what was intended (Ch. 5)
Formative feedback	feedback given to students during a discussion intended to improve student performance in real time (Ch. 2)
Gradually releasing responsibility	a process in which the teacher gradually allows students to take over the control and flow of the discussion (Ch. 1, 5)
Group cohesiveness	the resultant forces which are acting on the members to stay in a group or simply group members' attraction toward the group (Ch. 3)
Heterogeneous ability grouping	a method of grouping in which students of different ability levels are represented in each group (Ch. 3)
High-level comprehension	critical, reflective thinking about, around, and with a text (Ch. 2, 3, 4)
Homogeneous ability grouping	a method of grouping in which all of the students in a group have similar ability levels (Ch. 3)
Inductive reasoning	to build up ideas or tie things together, rather than breaking them down (Ch. 2)
Instructional frame	the set of principles on which an instructional method is based (Ch. 1)
Interpretive authority	indicates who frames questions and determines the answers to the questions (Ch. 1, 2, 3)
Interthinking	the collaborative construction of knowledge though productive discourse (Ch. 1, 2)
Knowledge gap	areas of content knowledge that students may be missing (Ch. 3)
Low-level comprehension	basic recollection of text-based details (Ch. 4)
Misconception	an incorrect idea or understanding that a student has about a particular topic or concept (Ch. 3)

Narrative text	a text written for the purpose of telling a story (Ch. 3)
Prior knowledge	knowledge that students bring with them to a discussion (Ch. 2, 3)
Reading comprehension	a student's ability to read and understand the meaning of a text; see also *Low-level comprehension* and *High-level comprehension* (Ch. 4)
Reasons	give support to a person's claim and explain why a person thinks the claim is right (Ch. 1)
Relational reasoning	the ability to distinguish meaningful patterns within dissimilar information streams; characterized by four different types of reasoning, including analogous, anomalous, antinomous, and antithetical (Ch. 4)
Scaffolding	a method of supporting student achievement by providing explicit instruction and/or modeling when introducing a new skill and then gradually offering less support as students master the skill on their own (Ch. 2)
Scientific discourse	a form of spoken communication, discussion, or debate in science (Ch. 4)
Scientific literacy	proficiency in the use and application of scientific concepts in daily life (Ch. 4)
Small-group discussion	a discussion in which a class is broken down into small groups of approximately four to six students (Ch. 3)
Social constructivist theory	a theory that proposes that knowledge is actively built during social interactions (Ch. 2)
Sociocognitive theory	a theory that proposes that learning occurs in social environments through the outward sharing of ideas and modeled behaviors (Ch. 1)
Speculation question	requires students to consider alternative possibilities and perhaps, though not necessarily, weigh them (e.g., "What if?") (Ch. 5)

Stance	the approach the reader takes during reading or discussion of a text and that varies based on the purposes or goals for student learning (Ch. 1)
Summative feedback	feedback given to students after a discussion has been completed, intended to eliminate misconceptions and improve future discussions (Ch. 2)
Teacher discourse move	types of teacher participation during discourse that promote higher-level thinking and productive conversation (Ch. 2)
Test question	question that has a predetermined and specific answer (Ch. 2)
Text genre	the classification system that groups texts based on shared characteristics, such as author's purpose, tone, and structure (Ch. 3)
Text structure	the organization system of a text that allows the reader to infer main idea, important details, and underlying arguments (Ch. 3)
Tool	a mechanism for learning (Ch. 1)
Verbal argumentation	argumentation that typically occurs during discourse, where one or more people have the opportunity to make or challenge an argument (Ch. 4)
Whole-class discussion	a discussion that includes all members of a class and is typically controlled by the teacher (Ch. 3)
Written argumentation	argumentation that occurs in written format that typically shows students' abilities to generate reasons and evidence to support a presented claim in writing (e.g., essays, scientific models, or diagrams) (Ch. 4)
Zone of proximal development	a theoretical stage in a student's knowledge acquisition of what they are currently able to do independently and what they are not yet able to do without assistance (Ch. 1, 2)

Contributor Biographies

Elizabeth M. Allen is a doctoral candidate in the Learning Sciences and Psychological Studies program at the University of North Carolina at Chapel Hill. Allen is licensed as a math educator (6–12) and a special education teacher (K–12). She worked at the American School of Yaounde, Cameroon, where she taught middle and high school mathematics and served as special education coordinator and teacher (pre-K–12). Allen uses a critical lens to explore how teachers' and administrators' implicit racial bias manifests itself within educational institutions, and its impact on student learning and cognition.

Chelsea Cameron is a doctoral student in educational psychology in the Department of Educational Psychology, Counseling, and Special Education at The Pennsylvania State University. Cameron's research interests include reading comprehension, content area learning, and learning from multiple representations and documents.

Rachel M.V. Croninger is a doctoral student in educational psychology in the Department of Educational Psychology, Counseling, and Special Education at The Pennsylvania State University. She is currently writing her master's thesis, which looks at the effect of teacher facilitation patterns during small-group discussions across student populations. Croninger's research interests include reading comprehension, classroom discussion, and teacher facilitation strategies.

Rebekah F. Duke is a doctoral student in the Learning Sciences program at the University of North Carolina at Chapel Hill. Duke worked as a research specialist at Virginia Tech Transportation Institute. She worked on projects investigating the factors that influence novice teen driver risk and parental influence on teen drivers' training. She also led the design of a research-based curriculum for Virginia judges to use in their licensing ceremony. Her interest in the nature of science and engaged, hands-on learning led her to the Learning Sciences program. Duke's research interests include scientific argumentation, epistemic cognition, and student collaboration.

Carla M. Firetto is a postdoctoral research scholar in the Department of Educational Psychology, Counseling, and Special Education at The Pennsylvania State University. She is currently studying the role of text-based discussions, particularly Quality Talk, in promoting students' high-level comprehension of text in language arts classrooms.

Mengyi Li is a doctoral student in educational psychology in the Department of Educational Psychology, Counseling, and Special Education at The Pennsylvania State University. She recently defended her dissertation entitled, "Examining the Effects of Text Genre, Prior Knowledge, and Perceived Interestingness on Students' Acquisition of High-Level Comprehension." Li's research interests include reading comprehension, content area learning, productive classroom discussion, and statistics.

Cristin Montalbano is a doctoral candidate in the School Psychology program at the University of North Carolina at Chapel Hill. Prior to enrolling in her doctoral program, Montalbano was a special education teacher in New York City for six years where she taught first, second, and third graders the necessary skills to achieve positive academic, social, and emotional outcomes.

Montalblano's research interests include productive classroom discussion models, relational reasoning, and executive functioning as it relates to academic and social-emotional competence.

P. Karen Murphy is the Harry and Marion Royer Eberly Faculty Fellow and Professor of Education at The Pennsylvania State University where she holds a joint appointment in the Educational Psychology program and the Children, Youth, and Families Consortium. Her current research, funded by IES and NSF, focuses on the role of classroom discussion on students' high-level comprehension of text and content (see www.qualitytalk.psu.edu). Dr. Murphy is a Fellow of the American Educational Research Association (AERA) and the American Psychological Association (APA). She is a past vice-president of Division C of the AERA and received the Richard E. Snow Early Career Achievement award from APA. Dr. Murphy is the editor of *Review of Educational Research* and she also serves on several editorial boards and has authored or co-authored numerous publications in outlets like the *Journal of Educational Psychology*, *Contemporary Educational Psychology*, and the *Educational Researcher*.

Liwei Wei is a doctoral student in educational psychology in the Department of Educational Psychology, Counseling, and Special Education at The Pennsylvania State University. She is currently studying the role of text-based discussion, particularly Quality Talk, in promoting students' high-level comprehension in language arts and science classrooms.

Page numbers in italic indicate a figure and page numbers in bold indicate a table on the corresponding page.